SABBATICALS
101

A PRACTICAL GUIDE
FOR ACADEMICS &
THEIR FAMILIES

BY NANCY MATTHEWS

NEW
FORUMS
Stillwater, Oklahoma
U.S.A.

NEW FORUMS PRESS INC.

Published in the United States of America
by New Forums Press, Inc.1018 S. Lewis St.
Stillwater, OK 74074
www.newforums.com

Library of Congress Cataloging-in-Publication Data Pending

This book may be ordered in bulk quantities at discount from New Forums Press, Inc., P.O. Box 876, Stillwater, OK 74076 [Federal I.D. No. 73 1123239]. Printed in the United States of America.

ISBN 10: 1-58107-149-3
ISBN 13: 978-1-581071-49-8

Illustrated by Mark Harper.

Photo credits: All photographs by Nancy Matthews, except on page 148, photo by Red Hill Photographic Rooms, Sovereign Hill, Victoria, Australia.

Although the author and publisher have tried to make the information as accurate as possible, they accept no responsibility for any loss, injury or inconvenience sustained by any person using this book.

To David, for your love and support, and without whom there would be no sabbaticals!
And to Lukas and Joshua, for your love, laughter, and enthusiasm for "Expotitions" around the world.
Love, Nancy/Mum

To the women in my life. – Mark Harper, illustrator

Travelling in the company of those we love is home in motion.
– James Henry Leigh Hunt

INTRODUCTION

My husband always reminds me that a sabbatical is "a privilege, not a right." Yet I can't help planning for the next one, hoping he'll be granted another of these perks of academic life. Not everyone takes advantage of these opportunities, though. Too many professors fear the upheaval to their homes and families, and just stay put. But sometimes all they needed was a little advice – information that could change a potentially stressful, unpleasant situation into an enjoyable and memorable adventure. That's where this book comes in.

After five overseas sabbaticals and exchanges, I've found what works — and what doesn't. Through the years I've made lists, compiled notes, and consulted other sabbatical veterans. Friends who were planning such a year themselves began asking me about sabbatical preparations, living abroad, and re-entering normal life. I soon realized I had information that could help both novice and more experienced sabbatical-takers, and thus began the seeds of this book.

Of course, my suggestions aren't only for academics. Anyone who sojourns for an extended period can benefit from the tips and resources assembled between these covers.

So I offer this to you as advice from a friend who's been there. Happy travels!

Nancy Matthews
Kitchener, Ontario, Canada, 2008

TABLE OF CONTENTS

Acknowledgments

Many people shared their anecdotes and advice, and without them, this would have been a far less interesting book! Others helped by proofreading, ferreting out information, or offering writing tips or encouraging words. Grateful thanks go to all these fine folk: Susan, David, Sarah, and Daniel Johnson, Marg Paré, Julie Falkner and Miguel Anjos, Sharon Kalbfleisch, Jock and Samm MacKay, Elsie Millerd, Lynn, John, Stephen, and Philip Rempel, Kathryn, David, Laura, and Khoral Hare, Rob, Nancy, and Heather Mann, Shirley and Jay Thomson, Janis Randall-Simpson and Bruce Simpson, Vern and Jane Farewell, Lorraine Atkinson, Marianne Ashborne, Anne Marie Mingiardi, Don McLeish, Wayne Oldford, Tom and Anne Wilson, Peter Taylor, Bruce Shawyer, John and Maria Brzowski, Philip Xie, Grant Holohan, Nandanee Basdeo, Margaret Gibberd, Sandra Gibson, Elizabeth Denbeigh, Rob Sawyer, Pat Forde, U of Waterloo's CTE library, Eleanor Anderson, Gini Gaffield, Shelley Brubacher, and Janice and Mark Harper (not only for great travel tales, but especially for Mark's wonderfully whimsical drawings).

Special thanks to my amazing publisher, Doug Dollar, and his staff for making this book a reality. And *most* of all, heartfelt thanks to my family, David, Lukas, and Josh Matthews, who helped with proofreading, editorial advice, moral and technical support, and much-appreciated backrubs!

Since my book deals with homes – packing up, settling in, and returning home – all royalties are being donated to Habitat for Humanity Canada in appreciation of the affordable housing they provide for people around the world.

PULLING UP STAKES

IN THE BEGINNING

You've been given the official word – the sabbatical has been OK'd by the powers-that-be and now it's time to get organized. You start by making a list: arrange passports and visas, price tickets, rent out your home, investigate sabbatical housing, make banking arrangements, explore school options, schedule shots, pack... good grief, what about the dog? Suddenly your stomach is in a knot and you wonder if going away is really such a good idea.

Stop. Take a deep breath. No one said packing up your home and family and moving to another location for six to twelve months would be easy. *But it will be worth it!* Just keep telling yourself that – and don't lose your lists.

Turmoil and tension – At this point I should confess that I truly hate the process of packing up and moving. In fact, the weeks and months before departure have been the lowest points in our marriage. There's too much to do and too little time to do it in. So, even if you're normally the cool, calm, and collected type (which I'm not), you should expect this period to be volatile.

Your children are not immune to this upheaval either. When familiar items around the house start disappearing and mum and dad become short-tempered, even toddlers can pick up on the negative vibes. Older children, of course, are more aware of the ramifications of the upcoming move and may exhibit signs of stress and insecurity, such as bed-wetting or other forms of regression, not to mention moodiness, defiance, and anger.

Helping the kids cope – While you can't snap your fingers and make all this go away, there are a few things you can do to help ease your family (including yourself) through this time of transition. First, *talk* with your children about what is happening, and *listen* to their concerns. Toddlers obviously don't need to know all the details, but they'd enjoy playing with toy planes and looking at books about airports before a flight. Examining maps and tracing your route will introduce your children to the concepts of distance and foreign lands. We even purchased a shower curtain with a huge, multi-colored map of the world for passive geography lessons. (Guests to our home also appreciated it; one gentleman returned from a visit to the bathroom exclaiming, "So *that's* where Myanmar is!")

Older children may be able to articulate their anxieties, especially regarding leaving their friends and pets or starting a new school. A year seems like an awfully long time to a child, but continued reassurance that they will be returning home at the end might alleviate some of their distress. Once you've started researching your sabbatical destination, you can hopefully ignite their interest with tales of anticipated activities and adventures, such as snorkelling in Australia, historical re-enactments in England, Legoland in Denmark, and safaris in Kenya.

Yo-yo time – Of course, this pre-trip period is filled with conflicting emotions for you as well – excitement about going, fear of the unknown (and what it will cost), concern over your children's adjustments and reactions, and worry over what you're leaving behind (house, furniture, job, pets, elderly parents, not necessarily in that order). Is it any wonder that you feel like an emotional yo-yo?

Unfortunately, even being an "experienced" sabbatical-taker does not make you immune to these reactions. As Robin Pascoe (1998b) notes in her book, *Culture Shock! A Wife's Guide*,

> There is simply no way around feeling stressed out. It's pre-departure culture shock and no one is exempt, no matter how many times you've moved before. Each move is different (like pregnancies) because the stage of your life, the age of your children, and the other human factors will have changed from the last time. (p.23)

The trick is to recognize that this is normal; it's simply a phase you're going through. You have to believe that this, too, shall pass, and you really will get packed up and start your new sabbatical life. Just hang in there!

PAPERWORK

Given the creaking wheels of bureaucracy, assembling your necessary papers should be top of your pre-sabbatical list. Even if you're moving within your own country, you should read this section carefully. Having your driver's license expire while you're living 1,000 miles away is *almost* as annoying and problematic as living 10,000 miles away. Here are some of the pieces of paper you might need:

- **Passports** – *Everyone* in your family needs his or her own passport. If you already have one, be sure it is valid until *well after* you return from your sabbatical. Many countries won't issue visas if the passport expires within the next six months. To renew or apply for a passport, check your country's passport information websites and phone numbers. Forms are generally available at post offices. (See *Resources* for details.)

    You'll also need current passport photos that comply with your government's tediously strict specifications. While you're at it, have a few extra copies made, just in case you need to replace a lost passport or apply for a registration form upon arrival. Start this process as early as possible, since valid passports are necessary before any country will issue you a visa.

- **Visas** – Most sabbaticals will require visas for the whole family. The best place to start is at the website of your destination's embassy, consulate or high commission. To initiate the application process, you'll need to find instructions referring to long-stay visas. If you're lucky, the site will have visa application forms you can download. You can also request this information over the phone. Just be sure you are incredibly explicit, emphasizing that you require a visa for a visiting academic and family. You should also verify whether these visas will allow the individuals to seek paid employment. In addition, if anyone in your family is expecting to be a student, make sure that this is clearly understood as well. (Often student visas require specific medical tests, e.g., for tuberculosis, before being issued.) However you acquire the forms, check them over carefully to be sure they are appropriate for your situation. It's amazing how unnecessarily complicated and confusing this process can be!

Start your inquiry six months in advance, but be prepared to receive your visa just days before you leave. My husband cynically believes that visa officials check your departure date and purposely try to cut things as close as possible. Expect contradictory instructions as well. When we last applied for visas for the U.K., the form stated that we were not to make any permanent arrangements until the visas had been issued. However, on the same sheet we were required to list a permanent U.K. address. Go figure!

If you call the visa office, you may also receive incorrect information. One family was flatly told they would not need visas in advance for the U.K., but would get them issued at the airport when they landed. They questioned this, but the official was adamant. That information turned out to be wrong. A horrific scene ensued at Heathrow Immigration, including frantic calls back to the consulate. Since the family had noted the time, date, and official's name during the initial exchanges, they were ultimately able to acquire the necessary papers. However, it was *not* a good note on which to start a sabbatical.

Frankly, applying for visas requires enormous persistence. Not only will the process be long and cumbersome, inevitably there will be some surprises. For example, you may find that only extended birth certificates that prove parentage are acceptable. If you don't already have these, you'll need to add weeks and probably months to the entire process. As well, be prepared for the post office, courier firm or visa section to lose your papers, followed by a request to re-send everything. If, by some miracle, you don't experience any frustrations in procuring your visa, just give thanks. (On the other hand, you can always think of the elderly lady on her first trip outside the U.S. When asked to show her visa at the airport check-in counter, she rummaged in her purse and proffered her credit card!)

- **Letters from the home and destination universities** – You probably had to produce these when applying for a visa. The epistles should be on university letterhead and be signed by the department chair, dean, or other such worthy. The letters should state the purpose and duration of the sabbatical leave and also the approved salary arrangements. Making extra copies would be prudent.

- **Driver's license** – Like your passport, be sure that this document won't expire before you return. If it will, see if you can renew it early or get an extension from the date it was *supposed* to expire, not from the date you call to renew. One fellow had dutifully extended his license, thinking the extension was from the original expiry date. Unfortunately, it wasn't, and he found his license was no longer valid when he tried to rent a car while overseas. After much panicking, faxing, and pleading, he was able to continue his trip.

- **International Driver's License** – Each time we've lived abroad, we've purchased one of these from our automobile association. When presented along with your current driver's license, you should be legally able to drive in most other countries. Through the years, we've never shown it to anyone, though, and have begun to question its value. Perhaps we've been in the "wrong" countries? Since it's an inexpensive piece of additional, international identification, we'll probably continue to purchase one anyway.

- **Discount ID cards** – The International Student Identity Card (ISIC) is a useful document for full-time students, twelve years and over. The card offers reductions on transportation, accommodations, and admission to attractions, and might save you a lot of money on airfares. Full-time teachers or professors can purchase an International Teacher Identity Card (ITIC) for similar discounts. Both cards are available from student travel agencies, such as STA or Travel Cuts. (See *Resources* for details.)

- **Documents relating to travel with children** – Be sure to carry official, notarized papers if only one parent is travelling with the children. (A template for a permission letter can be found in chapter 14, *Planning for the Unexpected*.) If you are divorced, you may need to show custody papers as well. If you are the non-custodial parent or are prohibited by a custody agreement from moving your children out of the country, you'd better get that paperwork straightened out early in the process, and carry those legal papers with you. If you have been widowed, take the deceased parent's death certificate or a notarized copy as proof. Lastly, if your child is adopted, you should include notarized copies of the adoption papers. This may seem excessive, but in an age of abductions by spouses and ex-spouses, you don't want to be challenged without proof.

- **Make sure you can come back** – If anyone in your family is not a citizen of your home country, you'll need to ensure that they can return. American residents who hold Alien Registration Cards ("green cards") and Canadian Permanent Residents who will be away for a year or more should contact their respective Citizenship and Immigration Offices. A re-entry permit may be required. Don't jeopardize someone's immigration status by overlooking this.

- *Carnet de camping* – If you plan to do some international camping, you might want to pick up this card from the automobile association. This can be handed over instead of your passport when you stay in campgrounds, especially in Europe.

- **Other useful documents** – While some travel books advise taking birth certificates and citizenship cards along, we've never needed these. Our passports have always sufficed. If tempted, you'll have to weigh the possible benefits against the chance of loss.

THE HOME FRONT

Organizing your home and belongings so you can be away for six to twelve months will likely be one of your biggest pre-sabbatical headaches. If your college student daughter continues to live in the house, you've got it made. You can *almost* walk out without any extra preparation. On the other hand, if you're renting out a furnished home, you'll probably have to clean it from top to bottom and box up many of your personal belongings. Even those who just close up their houses still have some pre-planning to do. The following are some things to consider:

Tenants – First you have to decide if you do indeed want to rent your house. Some people choose to leave their homes empty, with only a friend or property manager popping in periodically. In this case, you'll need to install timers and unplug appliances, and you'll want to check with your house insurance company for advice on maintaining your coverage. What you'll lose in rental income, though, you'll probably make up in peace of mind, since finding good tenants can certainly be a major hassle.

We've been very lucky; except for our first sabbatical, we've rented to friends and relatives, and even our first tenants were friends of friends. From the beginning, our goal was to keep the rent as low as possible, charging only enough to cover our expenses, rather than the market value. In this way, we could choose the people who would take care of our home. That's how we saw them, too, more as caretakers of our property than tenants who paid us rent. Most of all, we wanted people we could trust, so we reduced the rent to give ourselves choice and flexibility.

Once in a while serendipity will deliver the perfect tenant to your door. When Marg and François Paré were going on sabbatical, they facetiously said they were looking for a Francophone weaver to rent their home. Since both of them taught French, their bookshelves groaned under the weight of French volumes they preferred not to box up. In addition, Marg owned a delicate and unwieldy loom that she feared would be damaged if it was not used or dismantled. Their tenant? Another French professor, also on sabbatical, found through university connections. Yes, she turned out to be a weaver and spent the year enjoying both the Paré's library and loom.

So, if you need to advertise in the wider world, start with the university. Some professors have very successfully rented to grad students and visiting academics, while others can share horror stories (see chapter 34, *What Condition is the House In?*). One would hope that a fellow professor, who is likely also renting out his or her own home, would be a particularly careful steward of your property. Unfortunately, that is not always the case. But there does tend to be a correlation between how well you know someone and their potential as a good tenant. Certainly, if the person is not a close friend, you should ask for references and *check* them.

Rent – You'll need to settle on a price before advertising. Check the want ads to get an idea of the going rate. Even better, ask around the university to find out what other professors have charged for their furnished homes. Amazingly, one family found themselves in the middle of a bidding war. Two different couples wanted the house so badly, they kept increasing the rent they were willing to pay, but that is incredibly rare. More likely, you'll be panicking as your departure date approaches, because no appropriate tenants will have materialized. We were within two months of leaving on our first sabbatical when we finally found four students to inhabit our home. Prior to that, we were blatantly inserting "tenants wanted" ads into every conversation. Although we were becoming desperate, we were determined not to advertise to the general public. We definitely found that word-of-mouth got us the best people, even if that strategy produced results unnervingly close to the wire.

When you determine a price, you might want to consider incorporating additional expenses. One family included the cost of their biweekly cleaning lady into the rent. This meant that someone who was familiar with the home and furnishings was going in regularly. She not only kept an eye on things, she ensured that a certain level of order and cleanliness was maintained. Other families include lawn service or snow shovelling. Some landlords also require a deposit that is larger than a month's rent, to discourage tenants from skipping out with damage left behind. The deposit would not be returned until after the final inspection.

Lease – Whether you know your tenants or not, you'll need to have a lease. Ask friends for copies of leases they've used or just buy a standard form at an office supply store. Besides noting the monthly rent and period of the lease, be sure to state the maximum number of people who can live in the house, whether pets are allowed (and if so, how many and of what kind), who will pay for utilities and cable, and if smoking is permitted. Each adult who will be living in the house should sign this document with a witness present.

You can also compile an inventory of your belongings and have the tenants initial this as well. Listing each item you own is a truly daunting task, though. (One couple even itemized every book in their overflowing bookshelves.) However, if these lists also describe where everything belongs, they can be helpful for the tenants at the end of their stay. It's often hard to remember exactly where the stapler and the glass knickknacks were originally located.

The Tenants' Guide – Over the years we developed an electronic compilation of important household information. This *Tenants' Guide* (also humbly known as *The Source of All Knowledge*) includes instructions regarding house care, insurance, repairs, mail, bills, and even stain removal. We also list phone numbers for a plumber, an electrician, and the pest control people, just in case. The section on house idiosyncrasies describes locks that work backwards, lights that routinely flicker, and warns of a recurring leak in one living room window. The goal was to provide a sourcebook so that the tenants would know what to do in an emergency and would not have to call or email us with lots of little questions.

We revise the text each time we prepare to go away, and then print out a paper copy for our tenants. A condensed, generic, electronic version is available online at:

www.newforums.com/sabbaticals101.

It can be used as a template for your own personalized *Tenants'*
Guide. (A table of contents for this template appears in *Appendix*
A.)

The selling-your-house-first option – Of course, you could
avoid all of this by putting a For Sale sign on your lawn. Although it seems a bit drastic, one family has done this quite successfully.

As their sabbatical approached, the Hares decided that since
their family was growing, it was time to look for a bigger house.
They put their home on the market with a very specific closing
date (the day they would fly to Sweden) and a buyer quickly came
forward. So, pre-trip preparations for this family included box-
ing up and storing *all* their belongings and thoroughly cleaning
the house. Not everyone would want to tackle such an undertaking before a sabbatical, but it worked for the Hares. They had no
tenant hassles, no mortgage payments, and no concerns over their
belongings.

What they did have, though, was the need for a new house
upon their return. Dave and Kathryn pursued this by looking at
homes with their real estate agent before they left, and then keeping in touch via email. Thanks to the Internet, they also took
cybertours of potential properties. Returning early from their
sabbatical, they paused in Canada long enough to choose a new
home. With that behind them, they whizzed off to Hawaii for a
post-sabbatical, pre-move holiday. On their closing date, they
finally returned to tackle moving in, as well as re-entry. I know *I*
couldn't do it, but the Hares feel it's an excellent alternative to the
headaches of renting out a house.

If you're a tenant, not a landlord – Of course, if you're cur-
rently renting, you have your own concerns. Unless you plan to
sublet your place furnished, you'll need to give notice and find
somewhere to store all your belongings. Be sure to check a number of storage options, and ask for advice on how best to protect
your valuables. Alternatively, you could see this as a wonderful
opportunity to de-clutter. One couple sold or gave away most of
their belongings before going overseas, thus greatly reducing the
amount they had to store. Like the Hares, in addition to re-entry
angst, you'll have to search for accommodation when you return.

Dealing with the car – Again, selling your car is an option, especially if you were planning to do that anyway. However, most people hang onto their vehicle, so that necessitates a plan to keep it in working order.

The first time we left our car behind, we just put our old Toyota up on cement blocks in the garage. It didn't like that! When we returned, we found the battery was long dead and needed to be replaced, plus oil and other fluids had to be added before we could drive. So, on later sabbaticals, we asked our tenants to back the car out of the garage every few weeks. We left the gas tank full and provided an empty gasoline can, in case more was needed. (The vehicle couldn't legally leave the property, since the car's license always expired while we were away.) When one tenant confessed he'd never driven a car with standard transmission, he arranged for an experienced friend to regularly back it in and out.

Another possibility is to rent the car along with the house. You'll need to check out insurance ramifications and clearly establish in the lease who will pay for repairs, oil changes, etc. Be aware that if your tenants have an accident, the resulting claim could increase your insurance premium for years.

What to do about Spot? – While we spent decades without a pet in order to avoid this problem, some people choose to pack their animals along with their suitcases. One family drove across the U.S. with their dog, Snoop, who happily settled into their new home in Seattle. Another successfully travelled by car with a cat and a hamster, though, thankfully, not on the same trip. Unfortunately, some arrangements have less happy endings. When friends planned to spend four days driving to their sabbatical home, they arranged for a relative to put their cat on a plane once they were settled. Despite precautions, the cat ran away from the relative's house, causing much grief and a very unsettled beginning for the family.

Certainly, if you are driving within North America, taking your pet along is fairly straightforward. You'll only need proof of a rabies shot, a leash and/or pet carrier, plus assorted food, water, and litter paraphernalia. However, overseas moves may mean shots, papers, quarantines (check with the embassy), and travelling in the "pet ghetto" of the airplane. If Rover's along, though, you'll likely have a happier animal and children who may adjust better to their new location. On the other hand, having a pet on sabbatical can be a nuisance. Your travel plans and accommodation options may be severely restricted. In addition, the animal may not adjust to the new location and could even become ill or run away.

If you opt to leave Frisky at home with a friend, pet sitter or your tenants, be sure to provide explicit instructions regarding care (vet's phone number, meal schedule, etc.) and even stock up on food, kitty litter, etc. Whether Spot goes or stays, take your pet to the vet for his or her annual check-up and shots a month or two before you leave. If your animal is travelling with you, don't forget to pack up-to-date vaccination records. Otherwise Fido could be quarantined or denied entry at the border.

FINANCES

It's time to look at your money. If you're staying within your own country, things shouldn't be too difficult. You'll still need to arrange for your bills to be paid, and you may have to transfer funds to a local bank. However, if you're crossing borders, you should plan to ask lots of questions and make careful arrangements.

Bills – You will likely have some regular expenses that will need to be paid while you're away, such as credit card accounts, property taxes, and insurance and car payments. Arranging for pre-authorized, automatic withdrawal from your bank account to cover these will make your life *much* easier. Don't overlook annual or semi-annual commitments, like membership dues, magazine subscriptions, lawn services or snow shovelling, if those are to be continued in your absence. You'll also need to pay the final balance of your phone and utility accounts that probably won't appear until after you leave.

If automatic withdrawals are not an option, then you could arrange for a relative, perhaps a parent, to pay any bills while you're away. Other sabbatical-takers hire an accountant to manage their affairs. More and more individuals, though, choose to oversee their finances from afar, thanks to advances in technology. For example, while in Oxford, we began paying bills online, moving money from our bank to the appropriate accounts. Handling this ourselves allowed us to verify the charges and know that they'd been paid. As well, since mail delays were not an issue, there was less risk of late charges. However, if you decide to manage your finances in cyberspace, it's wise to pay at least one month's bills before you leave home, in case there are complications.

Banking – Start thinking about how you'll initially transfer funds between your home bank and your destination. One family swears by travellers' checks. They take $5,000 to get them through the first month, then open a local bank account and deposit most of the remainder. Another family carried a bank draft for $10,000, but after depositing it, found they couldn't touch their money for one month! Sometimes it's an issue of exceeding a branch's maximum amount (perhaps two drafts of $5,000 would have worked better), or maybe it's just a conservative financial policy. Due to our own bank draft delays in Australia, we had to borrow thousands of dollars at more than 18% interest for one month in order to pay for the car we'd found before our draft had cleared. All our careful planning was for naught. So, beware.

Our financial preference now is cash advances from a credit card used solely to transfer funds between countries. We deposit large sums into our credit card account, giving us a positive balance. Then once we get settled, we request a cash advance at a local bank. While this process of procuring funds used to be free, a charge is usually tacked on. We always do this transaction in person, armed with our passports as ID. The bank clerk then issues us the requested amount in local currency, leaving the balance ready to be withdrawn at another time.

Before leaving home, you should also verify that the PIN for your bank machine card is compatible with the overseas system you'll be using. Talk to your bank about this. If your PIN does not have the correct number of digits (generally four), request a new, internationally viable number.

One final word on banks – You may find yourself in a country like Germany where credit cards and personal checks are not routinely used for transactions. Instead, bills are paid by filling out bank transfer slips. "Everything from rent to concert tickets to church donations can be paid in this way," exclaimed my friend, Julie Falkner. "Even the beggar who hand-delivered a plea to our mailbox included her account number!"

Tax time – Brace yourself! Confusion over foreign tax laws is a common affliction of sabbatical-takers. If you earn any money in a country other than your own, you may have to file two tax returns, in your home country and at your destination. There's also the problem of trying to reclaim pension and tax deductions that have been withheld at source from any overseas income, not to mention untangling reciprocal tax agreements between the two countries. You may even need to file in multiple tax years. For example, while Canada and the U.S. use the calendar year, taxes are calculated from July 1 to June 30 in Australia. This means that if you're Down Under September to September, you'll need to file in two Aussie tax years. Of course, if your entire income originates from your home country, you have nothing to worry about. However, it can't hurt to confirm that you should file your usual form.

Since tax law is a many splendored (and much reviled) thing, you should request the appropriate government papers and pamphlets far in advance, and maybe contemplate using an accountant. Preparing and submitting your taxes online might also be worth investigating. Delayed filing is another possibility. American sabbatical-takers abroad can request extensions due to their unusual circumstances, and Canadians can postpone filing until they're home, if they are sure they'll receive a refund. Yet even among those who've followed this advice, there is much wailing and gnashing of teeth. My husband, a veteran of multiple, frustrating, and complicated tax returns, simply suggests, "Ask lots of questions, read the fine print, and expect complications."

Helpful tax guides, plus telephone numbers and websites for American and Canadian tax information, are listed in *Resources*. Good luck!

TRAVEL ARRANGEMENTS

Gone are the days when faraway travels always began in poster-strewn offices of travel agents. While you might choose to use these services, many sabbatical planners have discovered the benefits of do-it-yourself ticket planning. Thanks to the Internet, an immense amount of information is now at the disposal of the consumer, with no intermediary necessary. This is not to say that travel agents don't have their place. They can certainly help when things go wrong (airlines go under, flights are cancelled, etc.), but you'll likely have to pay a fee for their services.

Research your way to a cheaper ticket – As in almost all aspects of life, it's a trade-off between time and money. If you spend more time ferreting out good deals, you'll likely pay less. And while your time is important, no one out there cares about the cost as much as you do. Put another way, if travel agents get a percentage of the price of your ticket, where's their incentive to keep costs down? Why should they spend literally hours trying to work out a complicated, year-long ticket with numerous stops, just to shave off a few hundred dollars? That is why I've done most of the legwork when researching our family's tickets, bringing in the travel agents merely to issue them. (This is especially prudent in our province where, if an airline goes under, only tickets purchased through travel agents can be reimbursed from the special provincial travel insurance fund. Otherwise, I'd likely deal directly with the airlines.)

Where to start? – Before even logging onto your computer or assembling a list of airline phone numbers, get out a map, make some popcorn, and call a family meeting. First, ask some questions: Do you want to keep things simple and merely travel directly to your destination, or would you like to take advantage of free stopovers? Would you consider paying extra to break up the trip or tuck in a special destination en route? Where would you like to go? Dream big; you can always whittle your itinerary back to reality later.

One caveat: Think twice before booking a special stopover on your way home. If you're like most sabbatical families, you'll have been gone so long, and be so physically and emotionally exhausted, that you'll really wish you had just gone straight home. For example, we stopped in Prague at the end of our first sabbatical. I'm sure it's a nice city, but I can hardly remember anything through my fog of fatigue. I know three families who scheduled a final fling in France before heading home, and all agreed they were not in the mood to enjoy it. The Rempels even had a family meltdown on the Eiffel Tower. They had discussed possibly eating dinner there, but found it was too expensive. That prompted their twelve-year-old to throw a tantrum, and then his mother threw one in response! So, collapse on a beach if you must, but don't try to be super tourists en route home.

If you've been watching the ads in the travel section of your newspaper, you'll have some idea of which airlines fly to your final destination. (I start clipping these months ahead.) Beware of advertised prices, though. These likely won't apply to stays of six-to-twelve months. Sabbatical tickets seem to baffle airlines and travel agents, and that is why I've sometimes consulted travel companies that advertise in faculty publications, figuring they're at least familiar with the concept.

Armed with a list of potential airlines and stopovers, I then tackle the websites and telephone numbers. Phoning airlines at less busy times, like Sunday afternoons and holidays, helps. I also keep a good book near the telephone for those inevitable, long waits ("Your call is important to us…").

Since flexibility can save you money, check out alternative dates and routes during these initial inquiries, and be sure to note if taxes are included. You may be able to leave the actual return open, but more likely, you'll have to choose a tentative return date and then pay a penalty to change it. At least that's one advantage of these more expensive, long-stay tickets – you can generally shift dates or stopovers without too much trouble or expense.

Prepare for potential problems – Obviously, your options will be limited if you plan to use frequent flyer points or want to accumulate points on a particular plan. One word of caution, though – think long and hard if you have to fly separately in order to use a free ticket. One couple did that, saving a significant amount of money, but arrived home from Australia with tales of extensive delays, confusion, separation, and added exhaustion due to that decision.

Lastly, before committing to a particular ticket, be sure to verify what ages constitute children's prices on that airline. (The age should be based on the date of departure.) Don't forget to ask about discounts for International Student or Teacher Identify Cards (see chapter 2, *Paperwork*). In addition, confirm luggage restrictions on all legs of the return trip. Limitations on weight and number of pieces per passenger can vary depending on the destination. This is especially true when making stopovers while crossing the Pacific. You'll need to pack with the most restrictive policies in mind, or you might end up paying exorbitant excess luggage charges.

TRAVELLING WITH CHILDREN

Of course, some people would say there's never a good time to travel with kids, but I doubt they're reading this book. Since our family hopped a plane whenever we had the chance, I'm fully aware that some stages of a child's life definitely make the process more complicated, but that didn't stop us.

I'm surprised parents of newborns don't travel more; our eldest was airborne at six weeks. Infants are a breeze, compared with their slightly older siblings. They're very portable and just need to eat, sleep, and be changed. Sure, you'll feel like a Sherpa, toting an infant seat, diaper bag, and stroller, but since home is wherever you are, they don't mind that the scenery is changing.

Have toddler will travel – When we were planning our first sojourn to Australia with a one-year-old, friends thought we were either crazy or extremely brave. One book even stated that travelling with a child between eighteen and thirty-six months should be avoided at all costs, but that was precisely when we were dragging our son halfway around the world and back.

From our perspective, that just meant we'd have to do some extra planning. For example, we decided to break up our long, trans-Pacific trip with three stopovers. We also tried to time the flights to coincide with our son's naps or bedtime. Unfortunately, time changes and flight delays threw not just a wrench, but a sledgehammer into our plans.

At one point we found ourselves with an unexpected, nine-hour stretch from Hawaii to New Zealand during Lukas' waking hours. I dreaded that leg, and yet after we took off, he amazed us by lying down and sleeping for an unheard-of three hours. When we disembarked, a young man behind us actually said, "If I ever have a kid, I'd like him to be like yours."

Now, Lukas was no angel on that flight. We had to take turns eating because he demolished our meals. He left a trail of bread crumbs wherever he went (at least he was easy to find). He loved running up and down the aisles to check on the flight attendants, who gave him ice cubes to feel, taste, and drop in mummy's purse. He was especially delighted by the blue water in the tiny wash-rooms where we changed his diapers. (Parents deserve a medal for that.) The little bars of soap were a big hit, too. Frankly, I'm not sure how we managed for all the hours he was awake. But while the trip was full of frazzling moments, obviously it didn't seem so to our fellow passengers, for which I was grateful.

Unfortunately, this led to a perception that we were doing something right. So I looked at our next flight from Auckland to Sydney as a snap – a mere four hours. Ha! Lukas was *awful*. He wouldn't sleep. He screamed, cried, and knocked our food off the tray. He wanted down, he wanted up. In short, he was the child everyone fears they'll encounter on a flight. The only con-solation was that we'd never see our fellow passengers again!

Tips for flying with little people – With that experience still fresh in my mind, lo these many years later, the following are some ideas for making flights a little more tolerable:
- **Plan ahead** – Book far enough in advance to get your preferred seat arrangement. Some families covet the bulkhead with its plug-in bassinettes for infants and floor space for crawlers and toddlers. Others find the "baby ghetto" too noisy and restric-tive (e.g., you have to stow your carry-on items elsewhere, since there's no space by your feet, and the seat arms can't be raised, making it difficult to stretch out for naps).

    We routinely requested window and aisle seats for each parent/child pair, hoping that if the plane wasn't full, we'd also get the empty middle seat. When we travelled with only one child, the "off-duty" parent was even allowed some precious non-child moments in a nearby row.
- **Travel with your car seat** – If you have an infant or toddler, lug that car seat onto the plane, buckle it into the seat, and pop in junior. Yes, you'll pay for a seat; yes, your child will not al-

ways be happy to be strapped in, but he or she will be *safe*. Flight attendants used to lament that while coffee pots were required to be strapped down, babies and toddlers could sit on parents' laps. Do the right thing, even if it costs more.

A word of warning: Before you book your ticket, look carefully at the airline's policies regarding infants' and children's car seats. Only approved child restraints are allowed, those seats with labels stating they have been certified for use in aircraft. Just to be safe, though, print out the pertinent information regarding acceptable restraints from the airline's website and keep it with you when you fly. Thankfully, taking car seats on board is now a fairly common practice, so you shouldn't encounter the kind of flak at check-in that we did when our children were little.

Alternatively, check your car seat along with your bags and carry on a harness-type child restraint called CARES, Child Aviation Restraint System (www.kidsflysafe.com). The FAA and Transport Canada, as well as a growing number of countries, have approved CARES for use on aircraft. This belt-and-buckle device is for children aged one and older who weigh between 22 and 44 pounds (10-20 kg) and who can sit front-facing. Light and small, but providing protection equivalent to a traditional car seat, it seems like the answer to a lot of parents' prayers. Note: CARES *cannot* be used in cars. (See *Resources*.)

- **Earn points** – Register your children (even infants) with airline frequent flyer plans. That way, when you purchase tickets for your kids, they'll start earning points for future trips.
- **Reserve a child's meal** – When you book your seat assignments, look into special meals. Not only will the food likely be more child-friendly, your little one will also be served *before* the rest of the passengers. That way, by the time your grown-up meal arrives, junior might be finished with his.
- **Be prepared** – Pack extra clothes (for both you and the children) and lots of diapers in your carry-on bag, in case your luggage is lost or the plane is delayed. In a pinch, add a sanitary napkin (generally available in airplane restrooms) to extend the life of a disposable diaper. Include favorite nibbles, drinks (purchased after going through security), books, and

small toys as distractions, wrapping some of these to bring out when things get tense. Our kids also enjoyed listening to their own music while travelling; headphones must have been invented by a parent! See the *Packing for Kids* section in chapter 13 (especially *Pee-Wee Packing 101*) for more ideas.

Thank goodness for headphones.

- **To medicate or not to medicate** – Some parents give their children motion sickness medication in order to allay air sickness and/or to gently lull them to sleep. Our doctor once suggested this, but urged us to try it on a short flight first. We're grateful we did, as the medication had the opposite effect on our toddler. Instead of dozing off, he was soon ricocheting off the bulkhead. You have been warned!
- **Ear pain** – During take-off and landing, air pressure changes can cause little Eustachian tubes to become quite painful. So follow Vicki Lansky's advice (2004, p. 110) and ask the flight

attendant for two cups with wadded up cloths or paper napkins soaked in hot water and stuck in the bottom of each cup. Then put them over your child's ears (or your own, if you're having problems). It sounds odd, you look silly, but it really works!

- **Tag the kids and all their paraphernalia** – You may not want your child looking like Paddington Bear, but this is essential. While your infant isn't likely to wander, your toddler/ preschooler/child might. Attach a tag with your name, address, and flight information to your child, as well as to the car seat, diaper bag, umbrella stroller, etc., and don't forget Teddy! Sabbatical families travelling with small children are often incredibly loaded down, and it's all too easy to overlook something (or someone) when decamping.

Of course, many of these tips, especially advice on packing extra clothes, diapers, and treats, work just as well when travelling by car, train or bus. But no matter what your mode of transportation, the key to preserving your sanity is keeping your child happy. Of course, this is easier said than done when he or she is feeling cooped up, tired, hungry or bored. (Unfortunately, you likely are sharing these emotions!)

Bottom line, I found that being the "mum-in-motion" meant I became my children's in-flight entertainment: I read books, played games, fished out their favorite music, and periodically produced food and toy surprises from my overstuffed bag. I also learned to reduce my expectations. In fact, I abandoned all hope of sleeping or reading a novel en route until our boys were much older. I knew we had turned a corner when I no longer schlepped a diaper bag, and the kids carried their own backpacks filled with books, stuffed animals, journals, and music. My husband and I could even sit in a different row! So if you're travelling in the toddler trenches, don't despair. Within a few years, you'll reap the rewards.

INSURANCE

A s you prepare to go away, the last things you want to think about are hospitalization, car accidents or burglary. Yet these are precisely what you should be prepared for. You'll need to closely examine your current policies and talk with the various insurance agents to be sure you will be adequately covered on a number of fronts.

Out-of-country health coverage – If you're leaving your home country, you need to ascertain whether you'll still be insured once you cross the border. Some policies offer out-of-country emergency travel assistance, but only for short periods. If you will be away for six to twelve months, confirm the contents of your current policy (e.g., doctor visits, hospitalization, surgery, emergency medical evacuation), and if the coverage is inadequate, purchase a supplemental, expatriate health insurance policy. (See *Resources*.) Also, find out if you'll be reimbursed for out-of-pocket medical expenses, or if the doctor or hospital should submit the bills directly to your insurance company. Ask lots of questions; you don't want to find yourself in traction in Tahiti with no way to pay the bill.

Homeowners' and tenants' insurance – Run, don't walk, to your insurance agent when you've decided what you'll be doing with your house. Whether it's left empty or will have tenants, you'll need to meet the stipulations of your policy in order to be covered. Don't be cavalier about these matters. If an empty house necessitates someone coming in every other day during the winter to check for burst pipes, arrange it. There may also be a limit on the number of unrelated individuals who can live in your home, though this may be due more to city zoning laws than insurance policies.

Don't forget to inquire about your own belongings that remain in the house. You may find, as we initially did, that while tenants rent your home, everything you leave behind can be covered for fire, but not theft. However, we later discovered a company that only charged us a small, supplemental fee for fully insuring our possessions. Companies that specialize in providing coverage for faculty will likely be more amenable to these arrangements. At least they should know what a sabbatical is!

You should also ask about the luggage and personal effects you will be taking with you. Will they be insured for loss or damage, or will you need your own tenants' policy at your destination? Also, remind *your* tenants that their belongings are not covered under your policy, and that they should make their own insurance arrangements.

Car insurance – Talk to your agent regarding your plans for any vehicle you will be leaving. You will likely pay a lower premium if the car will not be driven off the property for a year. If you plan to buy or lease a car while on sabbatical, be sure to request a letter from your insurance agent stating your claim history. This piece of paper could save you a lot of money when applying for car insurance at your destination. (See chapter 23, *Transportation Decisions.*)

Trip cancellation policies – When you buy an airline ticket, you're generally offered trip insurance as well. Some people routinely purchase it, while others consider it a rip-off. A lot depends on how you assess the risk. A very expensive, non-refundable ticket might be worth insuring, in case of accident or illness, but read the fine print first. Is the policy primarily geared to short-term vacationers? If so, your extended time away may not qualify. Perhaps, for a small penalty, your air ticket already allows you to postpone your departure under these circumstances; expensive, long-term tickets often do. My advice is to pepper the officials with questions – you can't ask too many.

AN OUNCE OF PREVENTION
MEDICAL AND DENTAL ARRANGEMENTS

Pre-sabbatical medical and dental check-ups definitely should be high priorities on your to-do list. You want your family to head off in the best possible shape, to reduce the chance of problems while away.

Medical appointments – Long before your departure, book physicals for your entire family. Your appointments should be *at least* two months before you leave, to allow time for test results and further treatment to be scheduled, if necessary. Prior to one sabbatical, I learned that a routine Pap test came back positive, so I had to squeeze in outpatient surgery only days before we left. *Not* the preferred way of doing things!

During your check-up, be sure to note everyone's blood type. As well, have your doctor write new prescriptions for all medications, listing both the generic and brand names of each drug. Keep this information in your carry-on luggage.

Shots – Be sure to take everyone's immunization records to the doctor's office. All family members should have their vaccinations, including tetanus shots, up-to-date. Children's routine inoculations should be taken care of at this time. If they will come due while you're away, you should discuss with your doctor how these should be handled.

However, if you're travelling outside your home country, you may require additional needles. You should check with your government's Department of Health or your local Community Health Travel Immunization Clinic to find out exactly what inoculations are required or suggested for your destination, as well as other areas you travel to en route or while on holiday. (Note: Pregnancy may preclude some of these inoculations.) It is incredibly important to begin these inquiries months in advance, in case you require multiple injections or an extensive lead-time. So, don't leave this to the last moment.

Besides the pain in your arm, there'll be a pain in your pocketbook. When my husband and I were going to Thailand for twelve days, we spent more than $200 each on the necessary needles. In addition to the inoculations, though, we were given very helpful, area-specific advice. For example, we learned that while it was worth having Hepatitis A shots, due to concerns over food handling even in five-star hotels, we did not need to worry about malaria unless we planned to go way off the beaten path. You should check with your supplemental insurance company to see if they'll pick up all or part of the tab.

Resources and reference books – Cyberspace is another source for medical information and overseas support. For example, the Atlanta-based Centers for Disease Control (CDC) offer web-based information on recommended immunization and health-related travel warnings for countries around the world. (See *Resources* for details.)

Don't overlook low-tech references either. Pack a general children's medical guide, such as the old standby, *Dr. Spock's Baby and Child Care*, or other pediatric health and development books like the *What to Expect...* series by Murkoff, Hathaway, and Eisenberg.

Just in case – A basic first aid kit with favorite over-the-counter medications deserves space in your suitcase, too. If you're travelling to a developing country, you may also wish to acquire a sterile intravenous package. Ask your local hospital pharmacy to assemble a "traveller's kit" containing sterile needles, gloves, syringes, and IV bag. The one I investigated cost under $30. You should also request an official letter to be included in your passport stating that you are carrying these items for medical purposes, and then pack this kit in your checked luggage, *not* carry-on.

Eyes – Be sure to schedule eye exams with your optometrist or ophthalmologist, and don't forget to get written prescriptions for glasses and contact lenses, in case of loss. In fact, packing an extra pair of glasses would be wise.

Teeth – Dental check-ups should also be scheduled months in advance. It will be easier, and probably cheaper, to get routine examinations and major dental work done at home. Your dentist has your records and x-rays, and can anticipate potential problems. Just be sure to advise him or her about the length of your upcoming absence.

While you hope this type of preventative care will avoid visits to unfamiliar dentists, there are some on-going dental concerns you can't avoid, like braces. Ask your orthodontist for advice regarding your child's treatment schedule while you're away. He or she might even be able to give you a referral to another orthodontist at your destination. As well, examine your dental insurance before leaving to learn if overseas visits will be reimbursed, or if this will be just another cost of going away.

Important information – Lastly, remember to note your home doctor and dentist's telephone and fax numbers, plus those of specialists you may need to contact. If you're crossing borders, you should also verify the conditions and extent of your out-of-country health coverage. It may be worth purchasing additional insurance. (See chapter 7, *Insurance*, for more details.)

FINDING HOUSING

L et's face it, nobody likes looking for sabbatical housing. It's usually a tedious and depressing business with rare moments of serendipity. Not only is it difficult to search for a home from across the country or overseas, it's incredibly important to get it right, i.e., affordable, well located, clean, safe, and tolerable. Your family's happiness may depend on it. Needless to say, it's worth putting the time and energy into searching for an acceptable abode.

Putting the word out – One of our approaches to this problem has been to let *everybody* know we're looking for a home in city x, and then to pursue all leads. On our last sabbatical in England, for example, we had a surprisingly far-reaching network of people trying to help us. An Indonesian friend we'd met in Canada emailed us from Korea offering to contact his friend in the U.K. to look around on our behalf. Canadian friends gave us a lead on a small English business specializing in finding sabbatical homes (unfortunately, now defunct). We were also put in touch with a friend's sister-in-law's sister-in-law, and another friend visiting the UK clipped housing ads from *The Times* for us.

My favorite connection, though, occurred on a flight to London. A Canadian friend struck up a conversation with a British-born prof from a Quebec university. When Rob learned that the man was going back to clean out his recently deceased father's home, he saw a possible answer to our housing dilemma and put us together by email.

I wish I could say that we landed the perfect house through

one of these leads, but we didn't. Yet, with the help of these friends (and their friends and relations), we made an early start on our quest and got a good idea of the housing market. In the end, it was an online search for ads in our destination's university paper that led us to our final choice.

The Internet has certainly made long-distance house-hunting easier. While we ended up working with a rental agency, the Internet has allowed others to communicate directly with homeowners, swapping questions, stories, and photographs en route to signing the deal. Phone calls also help to flesh out the ads and to make both parties more comfortable with the arrangements.

No matter how you've unearthed your leads, once you've narrowed down your choices, be sure to ask your prospective landlord some very specific questions. Assume nothing, confirm everything!

The Basics – What is the rent? Is there a rental agreement or lease? How much is the deposit? When and how must it be paid? Who pays water, heating, property taxes, etc., and approximately how much are they? Are there any other anticipated expenses (e.g., maid service, gardener)? Are the arrival and departure dates flexible?

The Contents – Is it furnished? If yes, what furniture is included in the rent (beds, mattresses, desks, tables, chairs, bookcases, sofa, etc.)? What *working* appliances and equipment are provided (stove/oven, fridge, washing machine, dryer, dishwasher, microwave, toaster, vacuum cleaner, TV, VCR/DVD player, telephone, radio, CD player)? Are linen and bedding supplied (sheets, towels, pillows, blankets)? What kitchen items are provided (dishes, silverware, glasses, mugs, pots, utensils)? Is there a bathtub or a North American-style shower?

The Outdoors – Is there a garden to maintain? What about a lawn mower, clothesline, place for bicycles, garage? Is there on-site parking? If not, is nearby parking difficult and/or expensive?

The Neighborhood – What is the area like? How far to the nearest train/bus/subway? Where are the closest shops, library, and park? Are there children in the neighborhood? What are the schools like?

Note: While all this information may be incredibly useful in making your housing decision, remember to take some of the answers with a grain of salt. The landlord likely wants to close the deal and may paint a deceptively rosy picture, especially regarding the neighborhood and schools. If at all possible, confirm some of this information with a local contact. As always, it's "buyer beware."

The Accompanying Spouse

If you're the non-academic half of a sabbatical couple, otherwise known as the accompanying or "trailing" spouse, you'll likely have some expectations and concerns about how you will spend your time. Whether you hope to find a paid position, work long-distance at your regular job, volunteer, take classes, or be a full-time parent, it helps to be proactive.

Paying jobs – While it's often difficult to find a one-year position, especially overseas, it isn't impossible. However, you'll first need to ascertain whether your visa *allows* you to work (see chapter 2, *Paperwork*). Some professions travel better than others, such as teaching, writing, and editing. Yet even in these fields, you may be thwarted by extenuating circumstances, such as denial of a work permit, the local economy and unemployment rate, lack of language fluency, gender discrimination, or even unreliable mail service or computer connections. Any or all of these could throw a wrench into your plans. One friend, however, found a way around such obstacles. She wasn't allowed to work, but managed to find a job she liked. So she made a deal with the employer – in lieu of a paycheck, the company paid for her nanny and her mileage, which worked out well for both parties.

If feasible, another alternative is to continue at your regular job by telecommuting. While you'll miss the face-to-face encounters, the meetings (perhaps a blessing), and the conversations around the water cooler, you'll stay current in your field and your employer won't have to find a replacement. As well, this arrangement allows you to work around family trips, local holidays, and visiting relatives.

Flexibility is also a benefit for those who start a business at their destination. Freelance writing and editing, web design, translating, and tutoring are just some of the skills that lend themselves to home-based employment. In addition, children may find it easier to adjust to their new surroundings with mum or dad nearby.

Day care – If both parents are working, you'll likely need to arrange childcare. Word-of-mouth recommendations are best and locals can advise on the going rate as well. One family on sabbatical in Australia decided to put their four-year-old in day care, even though the father was working from home. After moving Down Under, the son's toilet training had regressed, and his days had no structure. So they signed him up for two days a week, giving him a familiar routine. While it blew a hole in the family's budget, they felt it was worth it, and the little guy even picked up a bit of an accent along the way.

Another thing to remember: if you're in a non-English-speaking environment, be sure you and your child can communicate effectively with the sitter. You need to feel confident that the person understands your instructions.

Alternative, unpaid activities – If by choice or default you find yourself without paid employment, consider these possibilities:

- **Continuing education courses** – Check out local community centers and universities, plus correspondence and online classes. Pursue an existing interest or try something new. Language, culture, and history courses are natural choices, but why not explore winemaking or the finer points of quantum physics?

- **Exercise** – Join a class and meet new people, or just jog, swim, skate or bike on your own. If you prefer to exercise at home, pack a do-it-yourself CD or DVD. I've taken my decrepit *Jane Fonda's Workout* cassette around the world for instant aerobics at no cost. (But I must confess that twenty years of hearing the disco version of *Bridge Over Troubled Waters* is beginning to take a toll.)

- **Family activities and travels** – Planning trips can feel like a part-time job. Researching destinations, button-holing anyone who's been there, and surfing the net for availability are surprisingly time-consuming. It can, however, be sort of fun.

- **Artistic pursuits** – Here's your chance to spend time painting, writing, acting, singing or playing an instrument. Unleash your creative impulses!

- **Volunteering** – Share your gift of time with others. Schools, nursing homes, hospitals, and a myriad of local charities would appreciate your help. Whether you give in time and cupcakes at your children's school, organize fundraisers for cancer research, or volunteer in your professional field, you'll meet local folks and gain insights into the culture, as well as provide a much-needed service.

- **Full-time parenting** – Of course, caring for your children is about the most portable career you could have. Whether or not you've been an at-home mum or dad before, the sabbatical will give you the opportunity to spend both quality and quantity time with your kids. One father was between jobs when his math professor wife had a year's sabbatical, so he enjoyed being the primary caretaker of their one-year-old daughter while in Australia. Actually, I found that country to be a particularly pleasant place to be a full-time mum with a toddler. When we weren't playing at the beach, we were off to local playgroups, where we met other mums and tots. We also checked out parks and museums, and became well acquainted with the library. Our flexibility also allowed us to travel out of town with my husband when he was invited to give seminars. Despite dealing with tantrums and needing to schedule outings around the almighty nap, it was a joy to spend so much time together exploring a new place.

- **Daily tasks** – Finally, don't underestimate the time it will take to keep the home fires burning. Small refrigerators will require more frequent trips to the store, laundry may need to be lugged down the street, and just getting across town could take hours. Heat will sap your energy, whereas icy conditions may make you hesitant to go out. But if you allot realistic amounts of time and generally reduce your expectations, you might even come to enjoy this different rhythm of life.

EDUCATIONAL ISSUES

If your children are very small, you can look for parent and tot groups or playgroups once you get settled. However, if they are school-aged, you need to start investigating educational options as soon as you know what neighborhood, or at least what town, you'll be living in. As with housing, the best approach is a combination of solid detective work and an aggressive interviewing strategy.

Your first step should be quizzing department members at your destination university by phone or email. Find out where their children attend and what options are available locally. Collect telephone numbers, websites, and postal and email addresses of possible institutions and get to work. In addition, find out if anyone at your home university has put children in school overseas, particularly at your destination.

Questions to help get you started:
- What is available locally in terms of public, private, and international schools? What are their reputations?
- Does the school year run from September to June or during the calendar year? What are the starting dates for new terms and when are school holidays scheduled? If you're investigating high schools, do classes run for a whole year or just a semester?
- At what age do children usually begin school? What is the birthday cut-off date? What grade would children your son or daughter's age normally attend?
- Are there any fees? If so, how much are they and what do they cover? (In Australia students on visas, such as children of visiting academics, are charged to attend public school. One year of high school, for example, costs more than $4500 Aus.!)

- Are there additional charges for uniforms, books, extracurricular activities, or transportation? If so, what are they? If uniforms are required, can they be purchased used?
- What extracurricular activities are offered, such as sports, music, drama, and special interest clubs?
- Is there a parents' group with whom you could correspond, or a keen, local mum or dad who could be of help?

Language decisions – If you're moving to an English-speaking area, you'll obviously have more choices. However, if the local schools are taught in another language, you'll need to decide if you want your children to be truly immersed. "International" or "American" schools might provide a partial immersion experience, where the local language is taught, but the remaining instruction is in English. In general, the younger the children, the more quickly and easily they will catch on. (See *Resources* for details.)

In many cases, you might be surprised by the rigorous expectations and high academic standards of foreign schools. Four-year-olds may be taught to read and times tables mastered two years earlier than at home. As well, the actual grades may not match up with your home school's. For example, "year four" in the U.K. is equivalent to third grade in North America. To help get your child placed correctly, include photocopies of report cards, sample essays, reports, and curriculum overviews when you ask the school to hold a place for your child. If English is not the main language of your destination, be sure to send translations as well. In addition, pack the original documents in your luggage, just in case the copies are mislaid.

Teens – You'll have additional concerns if your children are in high school. After extensive research, many families have successfully found schools that offered what they desired: a safe environment, the necessary intellectual challenge, strong extracurricular programs, as well as transferable credits. Interestingly, some of these students went on sabbatical not just reluctantly, but kicking and screaming, feeling they'd abandoned secure and enjoyable social lives at home. However, at the end of the year, these same teens left their new home, school, and friends with heavy hearts (and often tears), clamoring to return! If at all possible, have your teen talk to someone who's had a positive high school sabbatical experience. It could save all of you a lot of grief.

If your son or daughter is in their last year of high school, you might also want to consider leaving him or her behind to finish out the term. This, of course, requires a lot of thought and planning, especially regarding boarding and transportation. One mother who let her oldest child stay behind, described the experience as "wrenching," and said she wouldn't do it again. Going on sabbatical without one member of the family is a big step. If you're considering this option, don't underestimate the emotional component – for you *and* your child.

Special education concerns – Frankly, almost no decisions related to education are going to be easy. In fact, you should expect that the process of making school arrangements will leave you bewildered and frustrated. Unfortunately, if you have a child with special education needs, even more patience and perseverance will be required. Expatriate expert Robin Pascoe (1998a) flatly advises parents of children with learning disabilities to not even consider a move abroad. She feels that few overseas schools will adequately meet such children's needs (p. 138). Since special education dollars are stretched everywhere, a temporary resident who requires assistance or special lesson plan accommodation will probably not be "served" as well as at the home school.

Intellectually gifted children may also encounter problems if they are assigned to classes based on age rather than ability. While the whole sabbatical experience can be seen as "enrichment," gifted students need to be challenged on a daily basis in the classroom. Moving a grade ahead of his or her chronological peers or requesting inclusion in enrichment activities may help. But again, a temporary resident with special educational needs probably cannot expect to have them met.

Alternative educational opportunities may be the answer in these cases, as well as in situations where the family hopes to travel a lot. Correspondence schools, online learning, and homeschooling should definitely be explored if you have the time, energy, and especially, the inclination to oversee them.

The homeschooling option – We chose to homeschool when

we lived in Oxford, England, when our boys were eight and twelve years old. We had intended to enroll them in the local school, but were warned that students were only *allowed* to be away for two weeks out of the entire school year. That was too restrictive, since we planned to accompany my husband to Finland and Denmark while he taught short courses, plus spend additional time travelling in England and Europe. The boys couldn't even start school and later withdraw, because they would be "taking spots" from other children. So, we opted for the do-it-yourself approach.

I confess I entered into homeschooling with considerable trepidation. I certainly liked the *idea* (following our boys' interests, digging deeply into topics, learning English history through field trips, etc.), but didn't know if I could handle the *reality* (so much time together, my lack of patience, a totally different routine). However, I'd done some reading (see *Resources*) and made contact with an Oxford homeschooling group, plus we had our sons' teachers' enthusiastic blessing, so that helped. Most important, the boys were willing to give it a try. In the end, homeschooling was an amazing success and a highlight of our year together.

While we decided to have a free-flowing, interest-centered curriculum (except for marching through our children's math textbooks and hiring a French tutor), other homeschooling families feel more comfortable using correspondence or online programs. These can sometimes be arranged for a fee through your local school or school board, or you can purchase curricula directly from suppliers. This option is particularly helpful for high school students who require very particular courses (such as American or Canadian history) in order to earn credits toward graduation.

Even if you aren't planning to homeschool your children, you should talk to their current teachers and/or principals to learn what the schools would like or require. After such discussions, we were able to borrow math and French books for our year away, which enabled our kids to master that material and easily return to their regular classes. As for their teachers, we found them to be helpful, enthusiastic – and envious. Some suggested stowing away in our luggage and one hinted he'd happily come along as our tutor. So invite your children's present teachers to share their ideas and insights regarding your sabbatical plans. You might be surprised!

Homeschooling Oxford-style.

CULTURE AND
LANGUAGE
PREPARATION

If you're going to unfamiliar territory, you'll need to do some homework first. Boning up on your new country can be as simple as studying a map, as subtle as learning about body language, or as difficult as mastering verb declensions. But without doubt, the more you learn about the culture and language of your destination, the more enjoyable and successful your sabbatical will be.

Navigating the cultural quagmire – Thankfully, in recent years there has been a proliferation of books to help you. Country-specific series, such as *Culture Shock!*, shed light on daily life, values, and etiquette through anecdotes and advice. Other titles, such as *Do's and Taboos Around the World* and *Going Abroad – The Bathroom Survival Guide*, are even more specific. (See *Resources* for details.)

Books like these might just keep you out of trouble. For example, you'll learn when to shake hands (seemingly all the time in Germany, rarely in Thailand), and if you should blow your nose in public (never in Japan). Although foreigners will generally be forgiven their social gaffes, you can avoid offending your hosts and embarrassing yourself by doing your homework before you go.

Women, in particular, will need to be aware of acceptable dress and behavior codes. For example, bare shoulders are not OK on the streets of Bangkok, no matter how hot it is, and single women in Saudi Arabia can't rent cars, and must have a male driver. In some places, breaking local social rules could even mean criminal charges or deportation.

Women may also face frustrating sexism in financial institutions. When my husband went to open a (joint) bank account in Switzerland, he was told it wasn't possible. Instead, he had to give *permission* for me to write checks off *his* account. I was livid, until I remembered that this was a country where females in one region had only recently been given the vote. Frankly, it doesn't pay to get mad. You are a guest in someone else's country, and if you wanted everything to be like home, you should have stayed there!

Borrowing travel films and guidebooks from your local library will increase your pre-trip cultural IQ, as will reading novels set in your destination. A marvelous reference book, *The Traveler's Reading Guide – Ready-made Reading Lists for the Armchair Traveler*, lists annotated fiction and non-fiction titles by country and continent. It's wonderful to tell your family that you're doing sabbatical research when you're deep into a good novel. (See *Resources* for details.)

Unlocking languages – Preparing yourself for cultural differences is difficult enough in your native tongue. If you move to what one friend dubbed "an EFL environment" (English as a Foreign Language), it will be even more challenging. In that case, linguistic proficiency will definitely be your best ticket into the culture. While it would be interesting to carry on conversations about world events, you'll more likely need to communicate in shops or with your landlord. My goal was simply to make small talk while standing in line.

However, getting to that point requires real commitment. Only true linguists jump at the chance to learn a new language; the rest of us tend to clench our teeth and approach the task with reluctance or outright fear. The trick is to find what works for you. Books, CDs, computer software or online classes allow you to learn at home, at your own pace, but there's no one to correct your pronunciation or prod you along. A private tutor reduces these problems, but comes with a higher price tag. Alternatively, classroom settings provide increased structure and others with whom to interact. Another possibility is exchanging English lessons with a foreign national, such as a student, for tutorials in his or her native language. This way you can also glean information about life in your destination country. Try advertising through the international student office at your local university.

Before you tackle tenses and accents, though, be sure that everyone in your family knows some basic words and phrases. Here's my Top Ten list: hello, goodbye, please, thank you, yes, no, numbers one to ten, Do you speak English?, I don't understand, and last, but definitely not least, Where is the toilet? A friend suggested adding "Help!" to the list, which isn't a bad idea. Above all, I strongly encourage you to learn how to say, "Do you speak English?" in the local language. Even if that is all you can muster initially, it shows that you are a courteous traveller, someone who does not assume everyone in the world speaks English. Your thoughtfulness will be rewarded.

PACK LIGHTLY VS. BE PREPARED

I once heard of a woman who travelled around the world with only a small backpack, a black dress, black sandals, a black swimsuit, a jacket (also black), a toothbrush and toothpaste, a novel (which she exchanged en route), and two pairs of underwear, washing one every night. She'd periodically buy a piece of jewelry or a brightly colored scarf to perk up her outfits, but basically, that's all she packed. She chose black as her theme color because it wouldn't show the dirt and could be dressed up or down.

I admire people like that. In fact, I envy her. I'm impressed by anyone who actually follows the "Pack Lightly" rule. However, I'm afraid I'm more the Boy Scout type – you know, "Be prepared." Frankly, spending a year away from home means taking a few more items than you'd need if you were just travelling from place to place. In addition, while many supplies will be available at your destination, there are often some very good reasons for stocking up at home.

The following pages are a composite of past lists that I've used on our various sabbaticals. (Yes, I save old lists as templates for upcoming trips.) You might laugh at some of my choices or say, "I hadn't thought of that!" Either way I hope they'll help you decide what to take and what to leave behind.

THE LISTS

Adult Carry-on: The Important, the Irreplaceable, and the Just Plain Helpful

Note: "Carry-on" normally refers to unchecked luggage on airplanes. In this list, it also means "keep nearby" or even "don't let out of your sight" no matter what mode of transportation you use.

☐ Passports, visas
☐ Tickets
☐ Money belts
☐ Suitcase keys
☐ Laptop computer
☐ Health insurance information
☐ Official letter from university and letter of invitation from the receiving institution
☐ Letter from car insurance company
☐ Prescription medications
☐ Written prescriptions (for medications and eyeglasses)
☐ Acetaminophen (if you're travelling with children, you'll be lucky *not* to get a headache!)
☐ Financial information (e.g., bank branch name, address, telephone, fax number)
☐ Extra photos for visas

- ☐ Professional papers (e.g., lecture notes and research materials for the professor, articles and editors' notes for the freelance writer)
- ☐ Toothbrushes and toothpaste (to feel human again after long flights)
- ☐ Clean underwear and one outfit for everyone (in case luggage is lost or delayed)
- ☐ Travel journal
- ☐ Water bottle
- ☐ Camera
- ☐ Film – If you're still using film, pack all the rolls in your carry-on luggage to avoid the extra-strength x-rays that checked bags receive. In addition, always request hand-inspection of your film (some airports allow this). Make the process easier for security workers by taking the rolls out of their canisters and putting them in clear plastic bags. For further advice, check Kodak's website (see *Resources*). Alternatively, go digital and avoid the whole issue.

GENERAL EQUIPMENT AND MISCELLANEOUS SUPPLIES
- ☐ Extra camera lenses and batteries, plus universal battery charger
- ☐ Small national flag (handy for show-and-tell and national holiday-induced patriotism)
- ☐ Alarm clock
- ☐ Umbrellas
- ☐ Sunglasses, reading glasses, and spare eyeglasses
- ☐ Favorite CDs (including Christmas music)
- ☐ CD/MP3 player (battery operated or with adapter/transformer)
- ☐ Radio (battery operated or with adapter/transformer)
- ☐ Electrical adapters and transformers for all electrical equipment, including laptops and modems (available by mail order from Magellan's – see *Resources*; use their guide to verify voltage and plug prong for destination)
- ☐ Travel hairdryer (with appropriate voltage for destination)
- ☐ Photos from home (of extended family, house, and area to show at destination and to help children remember)
- ☐ Games (deck of cards, board games; *Tip:* To reduce space, pack the rules, tokens, and cards, but photocopy the board and tape it together at your destination)

☐ Coated hangers
☐ Cloth laundry bags
☐ Cloth grocery bags (in many countries it's BYOBag)
☐ Backpacks for everyone
☐ Needle and thread
☐ Swiss Army knife
☐ Most recent school report cards
☐ Most recent swim lesson report cards
☐ Car anti-theft device (e.g., *The Club*)
☐ Empty poster tube (to protect future poster purchases – fill with socks and breakables en route)
☐ Gifts to give – Think lightweight, flat, unbreakable, unusual, and useful, e.g., calendars with home country's scenery or art work, university t-shirts, tea towels, regional specialties (in my area, potholders or placemats quilted by local Old Order Mennonites), or the heavy, but often appreciated, scenery, history or cook books from your region.
Note: The obvious souvenir may not be the best choice. For example, we've learned not to give maple syrup unless we're visiting people who we *know* like it. It's heavy and can leak, but more important, we found that most non-North Americans don't care for the taste and/or rarely eat pancakes.

BATHROOM AND MEDICAL SUPPLIES
☐ Toothbrushes, toothpaste (see note below)
☐ Shampoo (see note below)
☐ Deodorant
☐ Razor and extra blades
☐ Combs, brushes
☐ Nail clippers, tweezers
☐ Shower cap
☐ Sanitary napkins and tampons (see note below)
☐ Band-Aids
☐ Anti-diarrhea pills
☐ Sunscreen
☐ Insect repellent
☐ Cold medicine
☐ Antiseptic cream

□ Home doctor's and dentist's phone numbers
□ Inoculation records

Note: Although not necessary, I've found that packing a year's supply of such items as toothpaste, shampoo, and sanitary napkins has its advantages. First, you'll have exactly the brands your family prefers. Second, the items likely cost less at home. Third, while these supplies will take up valuable space en route to your destination, you'll have room for the inevitable purchases coming home.

KITCHEN SUPPLIES

Note: Even when moving to a supposedly fully-stocked kitchen, we've found it useful to take the following items:
□ Vegetable brush
□ Vegetable peeler
□ Corkscrew
□ Cheese grater
□ Pyrex™ liquid measuring cup, plastic dry measuring cups, and measuring spoons (especially when going to countries that measure by weight)
□ Rubber spatula
□ Tea towels
□ Hand towels
□ Oven mitts
□ Can opener
□ Bodum™ coffeemaker
□ Paring knife
□ Cloth napkins, napkin holders
□ Favorite cookbooks and recipes
□ Insulated lunch bags and ice packs
□ Plastic cups

LINEN

□ Sheets and pillowcases
□ Bath towels
□ Hand towels

Books, School, and Office Supplies

☐ Address book
☐ Notecards
☐ Stapler and staples, tape, scissors
☐ List of birthdays and anniversaries
☐ Calendar (one with pictures of your home country can serve double duty for show-and-tell)
☐ Wall map (of home country, world and/or destination)
☐ Travel guides
☐ Foreign language dictionaries and phrasebooks

Clothing
(Obviously reflecting your destination's climate)

☐ Underwear (undies, socks, bras, slip, nylons)
☐ T-shirts
☐ Sweatshirts, sweatpants
☐ Pants, jeans, belts
☐ Raincoats
☐ Dress clothes (dresses, skirts, blouses, suits, ties, dress shirts)
☐ Pyjamas, nightgowns, bathrobes
☐ Shoes (dress shoes, sneakers, sandals, rain boots, slippers)
☐ Hot weather clothes (shorts, sundresses, sunhats)
☐ Cold weather clothes (turtlenecks, fleece jackets, mittens, hats, splash pants, winter coats)

Note: While it may be fun to shop for new clothes while away, it could be tricky finding sizes that fit. I discovered this when I arrived in Bangkok, and my luggage didn't. The clerks in the shops sent me to the Big Sizes section. This was disconcerting, since I normally wear a size ten or twelve in North America. In Thailand, however, I'm huge, so I had very few choices.

Sports Equipment
(Again, dependent on destination and interests)

☐ Soccer (shoes, shin pads, socks, shorts, ball – and needle to pump up)
☐ Hiking (boots, hiking sticks, heavy socks)
☐ Biking (helmets, bicycle pump, bike locks and keys)
☐ Swimming (swimsuits, goggles, snorkelling equipment, beach towels)

☐ Cross-country skiing (long underwear; we rented skis, boots, and poles at our destination)

☐ General (Frisbee™ – takes up little space, great for letting off steam, and crosses all language barriers)

☐ Camping (tent, sleeping bags, sleeping pads, flashlights, cups, silverware, plastic dishes, plastic dishpan, which all fit in one hockey goalie bag). To reduce weight and bulk, we borrowed pots, pans, and a camping stove at our destination.
Tip: Even if you're not camping, you might consider taking sleeping bags. They make great bedspreads and they'll allow you to visit friends without imposing as much. Unfortunately, sleeping bags cannot be used in youth hostels. There you'll need to rent or buy a "sleep sheet;" better still, sew up two sides of a flat double sheet before leaving home.

Packing for Kids – In addition to the previous lists, small travellers need extra, age-specific items:

YOUNGER CHILDREN'S CARRY-ON
(Pee-wee Packing 101)

☐ Diaper bag and LOTS of disposable diapers – Think worst-case scenario, such as your flight's delayed for a day and you can't leave the airport. *Tip:* Airline "barf bags" are perfect for used diapers.

☐ Extra training pants or underwear even for the consistently toilet-trained

☐ Plastic pants (added insurance over disposable diapers while travelling)

☐ Wet wipes

☐ Syrup of ipecac (to make a child vomit after swallowing something poisonous)

☐ Infant formula, if not breast-feeding (check airline's liquid carry-on policy for people travelling with babies)

☐ Snacks (such as raisins, Cheerios™, and bottles of water or juice, purchased *after* going through security)

☐ At least one change of clothes for you and your child (for the inevitable spills)

☐ "The Versatile All-Purpose Baby Blanket" – According to Vicki Lansky (2004) in *Trouble-Free Travel with Children,* this can be used "as a changing pad, to create a spot for napping, as a 'lovey,' as a nursing cover-up, as a coverlet for a crib away from home, folded for a baby's head rest, to pad a car seat or infant seat, and as a good 'floor area' for baby play" (p. 22).

- ☐ Feeding implements (spoons, cups, bottles, bibs, bowl)
- ☐ Front pack for carrying infants
- ☐ All regularly-used medications, including infants' and children's acetaminophen
- ☐ Thermometer
- ☐ Children's emergency medical guide (e.g., Dr. Spock)
- ☐ At least one sleeper
- ☐ Plastic bags
- ☐ Sweatshirt (for cool airplanes, cars, and trains)
- ☐ Books, toys, hand and finger puppets, crayons, paper
- ☐ CD/MP3 player with CDs and extra batteries
- ☐ Little surprises to bring out when things get tense (small books or toys, more nibbles, finger puppets, each wrapped up to prolong the suspense)
- ☐ The essential umbrella stroller
- ☐ Car or booster seat (with locking clip)

ADDITIONAL ITEMS FOR PEE-WEES

- ☐ Plastic outlet covers (if the plugs are the same configuration at your destination)
- ☐ Bigger clothes (your child will likely grow a lot while you're gone)
- ☐ Vinyl mattress covers and pillowcases
- ☐ Stuffed animals (limit the number!)

OLDER CHILDREN'S CARRY-ON
(Hooray, No More Diaper Bags!)

- ☐ Their own backpacks, well labelled
- ☐ Books
- ☐ CD/MP3 player with CDs and extra batteries
- ☐ Travel games, including a deck of cards
- ☐ A stuffed animal or two
- ☐ Their own journal and pens
- ☐ Snacks

ADDITIONAL ITEMS FOR OLDER CHILDREN

☐ Friends' snail mail and email addresses
☐ Lego (especially useful in hotel rooms; if you lose some pieces, it won't matter too much)
☐ Scrapbook with glue stick, scissors, and tape

Note: For more ideas, see *Resources* for specific books on travel with children.

A Word About Luggage – If you can't make the contents light, then at least choose lightweight, but strong bags. Our suitcases of choice are huge, hockey goalie bags – tough, strong, and a fraction of the weight of a traditional, big, hard-sided suitcase. Weight is particularly important when flying overseas, as you'll generally be limited by number of pieces, as well as weight. To ignore these restrictions could cost you dearly!

In addition, goalie bags are relatively inexpensive and, when empty, roll up and store nicely. Of course, one of their disadvantages is the possibility of putting in so much stuff you can barely lift it! Another problem is the flippy-floppy nature of a poorly packed bag. Eventually we learned to insert pieces of cardboard to make a firmer bottom, then to add a layer of books before packing clothing and other items.

For the record, on our last sabbatical, our family of four (with a piece limit of eight items) checked six goalie bags and one hard-sided suitcase. The latter held breakables and electrical equipment, and later protected souvenirs that we wanted to keep flat. We each carried on coats and backpacks, and my husband took his laptop and a briefcase with all the irreplaceable papers.

MORE LUGGAGE-RELATED TIPS

• Place name and address labels inside and outside of each checked and carry-on piece. Include your itinerary (inside), so bags can be re-directed if lost.
• Photocopy pertinent pages from everyone's passport, visa, ticket, and itinerary, and put copies in your checked luggage as well as leaving another set with someone back home, in case of loss.

- Pack anything liquid in plastic Ziplock™ bags and throw in extra bags for future use. They are invaluable and may not be available at your destination.
- Consult your airline's security-related packing restrictions for both carry-on and checked bags. Extensive instructions are listed online.
- Put suitcase straps around the middle of checked bags (available from luggage or camping equipment stores). You won't have to ask why if you've ever seen someone's underwear going round and round the luggage carousel. (But be prepared to have the straps cut, if security wants to see inside.)
- Speaking of security, use a TSA-approved lock that allows at least American officials to open your bags without destroying your lock.

A Final Note on Minimalist Packing – I'll never forget being on ground transport at Honolulu airport with my husband and two-year-old. We were on our way home after a year in Australia and had just hefted our full complement of goalie bags, plus one hard-sided suitcase, a diaper bag, three backpacks, a car seat, and an umbrella stroller onto the vehicle. As we tootled along to the next terminal, one man looked at our mound of belongings and exclaimed, "You folks sure like to travel light!" We chuckled, but afterwards I wished I'd proudly said, "Hey, we aren't on holiday; this is all we had for a whole year away with a toddler!"

PLANNING FOR THE UNEXPECTED

The best-laid plans often go awry. Of course, weather and illness affect travel arrangements, but I'm talking about something bigger. These events would be bad enough if you were home; add thousands of miles to the scenario and you have a proportionately more stressful problem.

Family emergencies – During one sabbatical, my father died suddenly. Telephone calls came in the middle of the night (enormous time differences wreak havoc in these situations) and lots of email kept me in touch with my family, but it was definitely a difficult time to be so far away. Arranging affordable airplane tickets at short notice was only one of the many obstacles to overcome.

While few people going on sabbatical actually work out contingency plans for such events, it never hurts to have a few *what if* sessions with your extended family before you leave. Would you race back to a loved one's bedside? Would you or the whole family fly back for a funeral? Could you afford it? What are the expectations of the folks back home? Sharing your thoughts with them ahead of time could avoid major misunderstandings later.

Wills – Of course, emergencies can also happen to *you* while away from home. Are your wills up-to-date? Have you made provisions regarding who should raise your children in the event both parents die? Nobody wants to think about such things, even at home, but the complications arising while you're living in another country could be insurmountable. Once again, some advance planning could keep a nightmare from becoming a complete catastrophe.

Money matters – A less dramatic, but still serious, concern is your financial arrangements while away. At one point during our Oxford sabbatical, I realized that if something happened to my husband – through death, illness or prolonged hospitalization, especially if he were in a coma – I wouldn't know how to access our money. He had recently begun using the Internet to transfer funds and to pay bills, and I knew neither his password nor the procedures for doing this. I realized how vulnerable I was and needed to be subsequently tutored in the ways of online banking. Thankfully, this emergency scenario never arose, but I felt better knowing I wouldn't have to worry about keeping food on our plates or a roof over our heads on top of everything else.

Permission letters – One last word of advice: if one of the parents needs to travel with the children in an emergency, he or she may need a notarized letter from the other parent giving permission. Airlines and immigration officials are on alert for child abductions by spouses, partners or ex-spouses, and could ask for proof of your right to take these children in or out of a country. Many nations now require such letters, so talk to your airline or travel agent beforehand.

While there is no official form, the following is a useful template, based on a sample consent letter (Foreign Affairs, 2008):

LETTER OF AGREEMENT

To Whom It May Concern

We, _____ and_____, are the lawful custodial parents of

Child's full name:

Date of birth (MM/DD/YY):

Place of birth:

Passport number and country:

Date of issuance of passport (MM/DD/YY):

Place of issuance of passport:

Our son/daughter, _____(child's name), has my consent to travel with

Full name of accompanying person:

Passport number and country:

Date of issuance of passport (MM/DD/YY):

Place of issuance of passport:

to _____(destinations) during the period_____(dates of travel).

Any questions regarding this consent letter can be directed to the undersigned at:

Number/street address and apartment number:

City, state/province, country:

Telephone and fax numbers (work and residence):

Signature: _____ (father/mother)

Date:_____

Signed before me, _____ (printed name of witness) on _____ (date) at _____.

Signature: _____ (name of witness)

THE DISILLUSIONMENT STAGE
OR REMIND ME WHY WE'RE DOING THIS!

As the pressure increases, so do the doubts. One friend emailed me three days before her departure lamenting, "Life is entering the 'why on earth are we doing this?' stage." Even the most enthusiastic person will suddenly "see clearly" and conclude, "This is crazy! No wonder people choose to stay home rather than go away for their sabbatical!"

Second thoughts – One year it hit me about two months before we were scheduled to leave. I was standing outside our house and started thinking, "Here I have a wonderful home, lots of space, and all our clothes and belongings to use each day. I have my own washing machine, I know my way around, where to shop, and where to go for help. I can speak the language and appreciate tiny nuances that foreign visitors would miss. I know where things are and I feel in control – it's so *easy* here!"

As I continued walking through my neighborhood, I noticed the trees, gardens, lawns, breezes, and birds overhead, and sighed, "I'm giving this up to pay an atrocious amount for a tiny flat in a densely populated city far away. No friends for the kids, no immediate support system for me, different doctors, even different shops and money, not to mention tiny fridges and expensive products." Thoughts like these can make you homesick before you've even packed a bag!

Even more negative feelings surfaced around midnight on our

last night at home, while we were madly cleaning and packing for a morning departure. Short of sleep and extremely stressed out, I had just made some grumpy comment about all that still had to be done. My pragmatic mother-in-law observed, "Well, you could always just stay home," to which I vehemently responded, "Right now I'd like to!"

The antidote – So, what should you do when an attack of disillusionment hits? I've found the best remedy is just to spill out your anxieties, complaints, and fears. Rant to the walls or a sympathetic ear, or scribble in a journal; just don't repress it. It's a bit like the stages of dealing with death: you need to go through the anger and denial before you get to the acceptance. Of course, this isn't a death, but a marvelous adventure, and in your less harried moments you *do* know why you're doing this.

It may help to list the reasons that initially excited you about going on sabbatical. Just seeing those in print should buoy your spirits and help keep things in perspective. Best of all, when the disillusionment stage hits again, as it often does, you've got an instant response to your exhausted cry from the heart. Just grab your list, re-inflate your sagging enthusiasm, and then get back to work!

GOODBYES

As your departure date looms, you need to gather the relational threads of your life and say goodbye. Those around you will "suddenly" realize that you are indeed leaving and you'll likely be barraged with bon voyage cards, dinner invitations, and goodbye gifts. Unfortunately, these very pleasant interludes in your pre-departure chaos come when you can least afford to slow down.

Learning to say "no thank you" – Dinner invitations are especially tricky. Before one sabbatical, we thoroughly enjoyed abandoning our long lists and relaxing with friends during that final week, but we paid for it dearly. I highly recommend telling people that you just aren't available during your last days at home. If they want to have you over for a goodbye meal, encourage them to invite you earlier. It sounds hard-hearted, but it's *very* wise.

There were a few angels, though, who said their goodbyes while rolling up their sleeves and pitching in. We also appreciated thoughtful friends who arrived bearing meals, so we wouldn't have to spend precious moments cooking. Others invited our kids over for the day, so we could concentrate on packing. Mind you, older children can be a real boon to have around. They can pack books and haul boxes to the basement as well as you can, and more hands mean less work. However, in the midst of your busyness, don't forget that your children also need a chance to say goodbye to their friends.

Easing the pain of departure – It's particularly tough to bid farewell to elderly friends and loved ones, not knowing if you'll ever see them again. Make the extra effort to spend time with them, repeating assurances that you'll stay in touch by phone, mail or email. And don't leave without collecting that data. Check your snail mail and email address books to be sure that you have current contact information for everyone you might want to reach. Encourage your children to request these details from their buddies, too. If you print up your sabbatical address, phone number, and email address, your children can give these to their friends, asking them to keep in touch.

Take photos of people as you say goodbye, so that you'll have these at your destination. Alternatively, assemble past photos of friends, family, your home, the kids' school, etc., in a little photo album to take with you. It's a particularly helpful way to remind small children who their relatives are, and can be useful for show-and-tell as well. (We always make sure there's one very snowy shot of our house, to impress tropical friends.) Include pictures of your pets, the living room decorated for Christmas, whatever tugs at your heart. Don't underestimate the appeal of this little album when you're far away. It will be a tangible reminder of home, and therefore worth spending the time to assemble.

Dreadful
Departures

We've all had them, departures, arrivals, and whole trips where everything that could go wrong, did. I include this section, not to deter you, but to give you an idea of how even bad beginnings can still lead to great sabbaticals.

Of Ph.D.s, Broken Arms, and Chicken Pox – You'd think preparing one's house and family for the big move would be enough of an undertaking. Try adding preparations for a Ph.D. thesis defense and you'll know how to spell "stress." Lynn Rempel was tying up the ends of a doctoral degree and had carefully scheduled her oral defense for a month prior to the start of her husband's sabbatical. On the day of her oral, her youngest son, Philip, broke his arm at school and Lynn accidentally learned of it during a pause in her examination. Her husband rushed off to deal with Philip, and amazingly, Lynn managed to remain calm and finished with aplomb.

However, that wasn't the end. Two weeks before leaving, her other son slipped in the bathroom and received a severe concussion that sent him to the emergency room and gave him splitting headaches for weeks. Then just prior to their departure, Philip's cast developed problems and needed to be changed. So almost en route to the airport, they made a pit stop at the emergency ward and later had the cast removed in Germany. Despite all this, they went on to have a marvelous year in Australia.

Another family was about to leave on sabbatical when their four-year-old daughter broke out in chicken pox. Since they had no leeway in their travel plans, they covered their daughter's most noticeable spots with band-aids and got on the plane. One wonders how many passengers developed pink, crusty pustules after that flight!

The Departure from Hell – We have our own horror story. One hour before we were supposed to walk out the door, it was painfully obvious we wouldn't be ready in time. I'd just gone downstairs and realized that no one had done a thing to pack up or clean the basement. I screamed for my husband.

Now, there *were* extenuating circumstances. Two weeks before we were due to leave, I'd learned that I had had a positive Pap test result. That necessitated a quick booking for day surgery that, unfortunately, was scheduled three days prior to our trip. Worst of all, "rest" was prescribed for the week following this procedure. So I found myself curtailing my activity precisely when I was needed most.

However, since it was D-Day, I decided to ignore the doctor's orders and began Desperation Packing, throwing things into boxes and stashing them in rooms the tenants wouldn't be using. Meanwhile, my husband literally emptied a desk drawer into his briefcase and charged upstairs. Once we were finally heading out of town in our patient friend's van, my husband asked, "Do you have the tickets?" Now, we were hardly neophyte travellers, but it turned out we'd left them at home, so back we went. But that was only the beginning.

Due to our tardy departure and a missed highway exit, we ended up arriving an hour late at the airport, and were met by lines extending out the door, thanks to an airline strike that was beginning in twenty-four hours. Mercifully, I was able to get a wheelchair (since by now I understood why I was supposed to be resting after surgery) and eventually we got checked in and onto the plane.

While the flight was delightfully uneventful, our 6:30 a.m. arrival was not. Our youngest son complained that he felt a little queasy as we landed, but I chalked it up to lack of sleep. Soon a wheelchair and attendant arrived to whisk me off to Immigration and Baggage Claim via the elevator, while my husband and sons trooped onto the escalator. Once reunited in the baggage hall, though, we found that while my husband was locating our luggage, our youngest son had thrown up on one of our carry-on bags. ("At least it wasn't the laptop," he later quipped.)

Thankfully, the amazing airline attendant who'd been pushing me came to our rescue. A roll of toilet paper appeared out of nowhere, and after some preliminary wipe-up, she swiftly took Joshua off to the nearest restroom. (I figure the woman deserved a medal for that!) Meanwhile, I cleaned up the suitcase and the family reconvened, ready to get our rental car. Ironically, that's how we began the first day of a sabbatical that, despite the cliché, really was one of the best years of our lives.

PUTTING DOWN ROOTS

IF YOU CAN'T MOVE IN DIRECTLY

In a perfect world, you would leave your home and promptly move into the accommodation at your destination. That's only happened to us once. If you, too, learn you will not have immediate access to your new home, you'll need to make some decisions. Basically, you have three options: postpone your departure, travel, or arrange a temporary rental.

Postponing – Sometimes you can easily delay your departure, but you should consider the consequences. If you're flying, you may cross from shoulder to high season, thus increasing the ticket price. You may need to get out of your own home to let your tenants begin school, work, etc., or *your* family may need to start classes or jobs in your new location.

Travel – Another way to use this transition time is to go on holiday, playing tourists at your destination or somewhere en route. On our first sabbatical in England, we dropped our luggage at a friend's and took off for two weeks of camping in Yorkshire, followed by a trip to Switzerland and Germany. At the end of that time, we were able to move into our flat in London.

More recently, we used the three weeks before our house in Oxford was ready for occupancy to make day trips from a short-term rental property near Reading. Taking advantage of our footloose state, we visited Stonehenge, Avebury, Coventry Cathedral, Kenilworth Castle, and several National Trust properties, as well as friends in different parts of England. We also bought a car, checked out our house-to-be in Oxford, and picked up invaluable maps and other tourist information at the local visitors' centre.

Housing while on hold – If you do need to find temporary accommodation, I suggest you again let everyone possible know your plight and even consider staying elsewhere than your final destination. Hotels or bed and breakfasts may be all right for a few nights, but for a week or longer you'll want something more cost-effective. "Holiday rentals" may be available in an area that would make a good base for memorable day-trips. Use the inconvenience of not being able to move in as an opportunity to do some exploring. You may find that being on hold isn't such a bad thing after all.

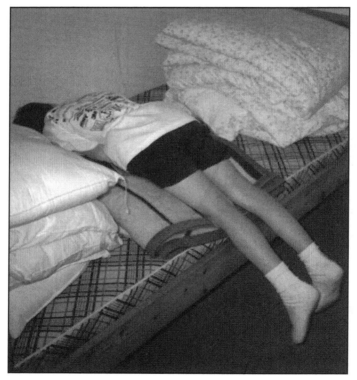

The joys of jet lag.

THE SETTLING-IN BLUES

It doesn't matter how organized you are or how often you've gone on sabbatical, there comes a time soon after moving into your permanent lodging that it all becomes "too much." Too much change, too many decisions to make, too many things to do, too much uncertainty. The list is different for everyone, but the reaction is often the same: feelings of inadequacy, frustration, anger, and probably some tears.

Pity party time – One memorable "Waterloo" came on the third morning after moving into our permanent home in Oxford. I hadn't slept well and by 3 a.m. I was contemplating getting up and making a list of all the things that were going wrong. I could later acknowledge that the list ranged from the petty to the pathetic, but I was never more in earnest than in the wee hours of that morning. Stores, heating, appliance repairs, concerns about the children – this mental list (thankfully, it never made the leap onto paper until now) grew and grew.

Finally, when my husband got up at 5 a.m., I was ready to explode and proceeded to invite him to my pity party. I ranted, raved, sulked, and lamented for almost an hour before I could feel a sense of normalcy returning. My ever-patient husband quietly listened, then made a few select comments that brought some perspective to a very over-the-top situation.

Transitional fatigue – I knew after reading books on overseas living and talking to other sabbatical veterans, though, that I was not alone in my reaction. Those first few days and weeks can be pretty overwhelming. Your body is out of whack if you crossed time zones; you may feel disoriented by the differences in food, pace of life or language; you don't know where to find things or how to get around. In short, you no longer feel like the competent and in-control adult you normally are. Diagnosis: you're suffering from "culture shock."

In his book, *Survival Kit for Overseas Living*, L. Robert Kohls (2001) defines culture shock as "the term used to describe the more pronounced reactions to the psychological disorientation most people experience when they move for an extended period of time into a culture markedly different from their own" (p. 91). He also notes, "Culture shock can cause intense discomfort, often accompanied by hyperirritability, bitterness, resentment, homesickness, and depression. In some cases distinct physical symptoms of psychosomatic illness occur" (p. 92).

While culture shock is most obvious when you move overseas, you can take a sabbatical within your own country and feel out of sync. Even if the currency hasn't changed, the shops, accents or ways of doing things may not be what you're used to. Plus, it simply takes time to shift from the normal routines of life and work at home to a new, long-term, but temporary existence in another place. You will need to feel your way, ask questions, and look foolish before you can develop a sense of belonging and competence. Here are some things that will help:

• **Be gentle with yourself** – Reduce your expectations of yourself, your family, and the new locale, and ease into life slowly. Go for walks, read a good novel, give yourself time.

• **Collect information** – If you feel, as I do, that "information is power," then pick up all the flyers, free maps, ads, and tourist brochures you can. I may have overdone this, though, since my husband regularly lamented, "More paper?!" An expanding file or even some large envelopes will help tame (and hide) your collection. However, I constantly referred to these bits of paper during our time away. And yes, in the end we schlepped a good deal of it home, much to my husband's chagrin.

- **Make connections** – One couple didn't wait to be invited for a meal by their new colleagues; instead, they asked people in the department to dinner soon after arriving. That way, they immediately made some local contacts and were almost assured of return invitations!

Are you a member of a group back home, such as Rotary, Optimist or Kinsmen? See if there is a local branch. Or are you a bird-watcher, stamp collector or astronomy buff? Search the telephone directory or check at the local library for meetings of kindred spirits. Joining a sports team is another idea. One Canadian on sabbatical in Australia played on an expatriate hockey team. He then travelled around the country competing against other expat teams.

Our family always searches for a local church when we move to a new location. Even if it's only for six months, we jump in with both feet, attending worship services, joining study groups, and sending the kids to the children's program. We have made life-long friends this way and have enjoyed worshipping with others around the world.

Some universities have "newcomers' clubs" that offer friendship, outings, information, speakers, and even weekly mums and tots groups for graduate students, visiting academics, and their families. Oxford University has a very popular and well-established organization through which I toured some of the medieval colleges, learned about Morris dancing, and met other foreign visitors. The Newcomers' Club also organized special interest groups for avid gardeners, walkers, and book club members.

Another international possibility is expatriate groups. When Sharon Kalbfleisch, a Canadian friend, lived in Belgium, she discovered the American Club, which was filled with women who shared much-needed advice on adjusting to life there. After that positive experience, she sought out the American Club in Singapore, calling it a "critical place for people wanting to make connections." She gleaned many invaluable travel tips through this group, and was even able to give back to the organization by leading a workshop.

Unfortunately, one of the drawbacks of expat groups is that they can be rather insular. Singapore also had a Canadian Club, but Sharon found it to be not only smaller and more reserved than the American Club, but dedicated to "being Canadian and doing Canadian things." While this can provide a much-appreciated touchstone with home, it can also degenerate into weekly "us and them" gripe sessions. Nevertheless, these groups are worth seeking out for whatever support they may be able to provide.

- **Consult the consulates** – Don't forget the consulates or embassies. Check their websites or visit in person to learn about local expatriate activities and contacts, plus additional services. In Berne, Switzerland, we discovered a wonderful, small English library in the basement of the British embassy. It became my salvation during our six-month stint in that German-speaking part of Switzerland.

- **Get oriented** – Use a map, not the freebie from the tourist office, but a detailed, local directory to help you navigate. I picked up a street index map when we first moved to Newcastle, Australia, so I could stake out the roundabouts. Since I dreaded these alternative intersections, I wanted to be prepared. In fact, I grew so dependent on this guide that I searched for one for my community when I returned home.

- **Change your mindset** – When the cultural disorientation and fatigue start to get to you, remember that the way the locals do things isn't wrong, just different. A friend who's a substitute teacher helped me to understand the difference. Whenever she's in a new class, her students inevitably announce that she's doing something incorrectly. Each time she replies that what she's doing isn't wrong, just different. I remembered her comment when I was irritated after stopping at my local English postal outlet. It was closed over lunch, so the employee could eat. This seemed a strange way to do business, but it reflected the local priorities. It wasn't wrong, just different. I decided that wasn't a bad mantra for those first weeks and months, and indeed, for life in general.

- **Keep a sense of humor** – Lastly, when in doubt, laugh. If you can step outside a particularly frustrating situation and chuckle instead of scream, you'll be that much further ahead.

Finally feeling settled – After weeks or, more likely, months of telling people you're slowly adjusting, there comes a time when you realize that you've settled. Often that moment of revelation occurs when you're out in your new town and observe someone else who is obviously new, confused or just a tourist. I stood on an Oxford street one day and thought, I LIVE here. I know the shortcuts through the back streets, which buses to take, which line to get into, and (my real coup) where to find the cheapest postcards. OK, so buying postcards showed I really wasn't a local, but that sense of having insider knowledge gleaned from weeks of experimenting, making mistakes, and learning whom and what to ask, suddenly coalesced into renewed confidence and energy. Not surprisingly, my 5 a.m. catharsis of three months before simply felt like a bad dream.

HELPING YOUR TEENS

You could face additional adjustment problems if you've moved a reluctant (or angry) teenager. Twin fifteen-year-old sisters arrived in San Francisco on a gorgeous, sunny day and proceeded to criticize everything, including the weather and the architecture ("The houses look stupid.") Another teenaged girl had trouble adjusting to her reduced standard of living in jolly olde England. She exclaimed over the condition of the musty, furnished row house, lamenting the large, modern home she'd left behind. Another teen was so unhappy about moving that she was allowed to have a friend fly with her to New Zealand for the first few weeks, to help the transition. Her father felt it was an expensive, but successful way out of a tricky situation. A mother of yet more teenaged girls flatly advises parents to ignore their offspring's complaints and just go, saying that these same teens will likely cry when they have to return home. As the mother of the twins put it, "Oh, man, they didn't want to go; oh, man, they didn't want to come home!"

I don't know if this is a female phenomenon, but all the stories I've heard have been about daughters. Maybe teenaged boys go with the flow a little better. Certainly our oldest son loved our year away, and even tried to convince another boy, whose parents were considering going overseas, to embrace the opportunity. "It was the best year of my life!" he enthused. While those of us present chuckled at this "aged" fourteen-year-old's exclamation, it was clear he meant it.

If you want to increase the chance that your teenagers will have a positive and memorable sabbatical, look for ways to help them make their own connections:

• **Introduce them to other teens** – If you're in an expat community, ferret out teens who've already settled in, and who can show your son or daughter some of the positive aspects of overseas life. Be sure they meet some local young people, too. These relationships may produce some of the best memories of their time away.

- **Encourage involvement** – Investigate sports or special interest groups, such as community drama, art, music or cooking classes.
- **Research volunteer opportunities** – Although they may not be able to work while on sabbatical due to age or visa restrictions, teens can gain valuable experience volunteering. As well, during one year away, our youngest son was able to complete the forty hours of community service his home high school required to graduate. (In later job interviews Josh was often asked about his unusual résumé entry, "Cared for koalas at an Australian nature park.") Students might also enjoy trying out a career by job shadowing.

Josh with Susie, the koala.

- **Investigate jobs** – Informal employment, such as babysitting, painting a friend's boat, or helping with computer problems, may be another possibility. Brainstorm with your child, and then pass the word that your teen is interested and available.
- **Encourage independent mobility** – Since some teens with licenses may not be able to drive in their new locales, help them to become transit savvy, so they can get around independently. Buying bus passes or a bike could save many headaches and reduce the need for you to play taxi driver.
- **Help them learn the lingo** – If English is not spoken on the street, language classes will also help your teen feel less dependent on you. Enrolling in a conversation class will offer opportunities to feel more comfortable when out on their own, and provide an easy way to meet other foreigners.

Bottom line, whether your teenagers came willingly or feel they've been dragged across the world, be proactive in helping them to settle in. Your whole family will benefit.

Moving In and
Stocking Up

Depending on your housing arrangements, you may need to purchase supplemental supplies soon after arriving. These can range from tea towels and a bread knife to major pieces of furniture. When the Jarrett family came to Canada from Australia for a year, they were unable to find furnished accommodation and were forced to rent a totally empty townhouse. All the people in my husband's department dug through their attics and produced linen, tables, chairs, pots, and pans, etc. The family bought dishes and glassware and rented a TV, but whenever guests were invited for dinner, they were requested to bring chairs, dishes, and silverware for themselves. It wasn't a perfect arrangement, but it worked.

Furnished/unfurnished – Thankfully, most people don't face quite so bleak a situation upon arrival. Personal experience, though, has led my husband to conclude that, "The word 'furnished' is an adjective whose meaning is only precisely understood when preceded by the prefix 'un.'" Even if you're lucky enough to receive a property inventory before you leave home, that doesn't mean that everything listed will be present or functional when you arrive, especially in the kitchen. As I mentioned in the packing section, we always take some basics, such as a can opener, scissors, and a sharp knife, just in case.

On each of our sabbaticals we were lucky enough to have local friends who could lend us things, like extra blankets, children's toys, and a card table. When the Paré family was in Holland, a Dutch friend loaned them a tiny washing machine, since their apartment building had no laundry facilities and laundromats didn't exist in their town. This strange, counter-top model rotated in only one direction, but it was better than washing everything by hand.

Buying used – If you do need to supplement your provisions, think "garage sale." In England that meant looking for "jumble sales," "boot sales" (not footwear, but stuff sold from the trunk of a car), and "charity shops" which sold not only used clothing and books, but also kitchen items. Best of all were special used equipment sales associated with university newcomers' clubs. In Oxford we were able to purchase a desk lamp, plastic containers, clocks, wine glasses, and even a child's bike, all left behind by previous international visitors. Since prices were half or a third of what we'd have paid in a store, it's worth asking if anything similar exists in your new community.

Keeping the supply lines open – You can also have someone at home send you provisions, although that can get pricey. The Hares knew that their daughters, who were voracious readers, would quickly exhaust the local supply of English books at their destination. So before leaving for a year in Sweden, they boxed up books and arranged for a relative to mail them every few months. These were later donated to the children's school and local library, where they were gratefully accepted.

Mid-sabbatical trips to North America also offer a chance to stock up on forgotten, hard-to-find or expensive items. When I had to fly to Seattle after my father died, I took an empty, hard-sided suitcase. Heading back to England, it held some shampoo and books I'd picked up, plus seven large containers of peanut butter, enough to last our family until the end of our stay. My boys had really missed this item, since we rarely bought it due to its exorbitant price. (At that time, peanut butter cost almost three times more in England than at home.) So when I arrived, I don't know whether the kids were happier to see me or the peanut butter!

BUREAUCRATIC HASSLES AND INITIAL EXPENSES

Within days of moving in, you'll need to tackle "officialdom." It can't be avoided; you'll have to be registered, stamped, approved, and connected if you want to receive the services of the local community, and perhaps even to reside there legally.

Battling the bureaucracies – If while entering the country you were told to register with the local police, then do so promptly. This often reflects the restrictions on your visa or your country of origin. You might also be required to fill out a residence permit form, which, if it's not in English, can be an exercise in patience. My Kiwi friend, Julie Falkner, encountered this situation after moving to Germany:

> We had an interesting couple of hours at the library using a big dictionary to help translate the residence permit form. Later I looked up some notes in my Germany folder to help understand the remaining questions, e.g., 'Income tax bracket?' We're all set now – except that we can't get a residence permit until we have a place to live, and we can't activate our work permits without a residence permit...

The Hares found themselves in a similar Catch-22 in Sweden. They needed a "person number" to do anything in that country, e.g., banking, paying the dentist or registering for school. However, to get a number, one needed to reside in the country for a year. (They were leaving after eleven months.) Eventually, the Hares were able to buy a car and open a bank account, by saying they were staying for twelve months. They also arranged to rent a musical instrument. Of the car, bank account, and instrument rental, the latter was the most difficult, since one must live in Sweden for *three* years before that is normally possible. In this case, a friend came to the rescue and rented the electric piano in his name.

Domestic arrangements and expenses – If you can claw your way out of such bureaucratic morasses, you'll then need to get your telephone and utilities hooked up. Depending on where you live, you could wait minutes or months. On our first sabbatical in London in 1983, it took seven weeks and numerous return visits to British Telecom to get a working telephone. But fifteen years later, we had almost instant service after just one phone call.

Likewise, arrangements for cable hook-up may be straightforward, but check with your local contact for unexpected expenses. In England we got hit with an annual TV license fee. (At least they no longer charge for owning a radio.) You pay less if your "telly" is black and white, but without a license, you'll receive a hefty fine if caught by the mobile TV detectors.

It's worth comparing Internet Service Providers (ISP) before leaving home. My husband recommends (only somewhat facetiously) that if you're used to high speed, consider downloading all the information you'll need in the coming year before you leave home. North Americans tend to be spoiled by very fast broadband services, so you may need to adjust your expectations abroad.

Hired Hands – A totally different type of household expense is the paid staff that may come with your abode. Our rent in Australia included the continued services of a gardener (and a very interesting and competent chap he was). Others have found that cleaning staff were part and parcel of their tenants' agreement. That could be anything from a firm that comes in twice a month to a live-in maid. People who have never before employed servants may find this a little difficult to adjust to. Since I have not dealt with this situation, I defer to those more experienced. According to Monica Rabe (1997),

> You cannot expect your domestic employees to share your cultural values. They might learn from you and at best, you will learn from them. When giving instructions to servants, be explicit, talk slowly and make

them repeat what you have said. Remember that in many Asian cultures, for example, people must never say no in order not to 'lose face.' They will thus always answer yes even if they do not understand. Finally, avoid confrontations and keep your temper! (p. 97)

One friend on sabbatical in Singapore was baffled and exasperated by her cleaning lady, who continuously mopped the spotless floors and seemed perpetually grumpy. My friend experienced what author Robin Pascoe (1998b) has dubbed "servant culture shock." Quips Pascoe, "You can't have your maid and privacy too" (p. 120). She suggests talking to other expats for advice regarding expectations, responsibilities, payment, and the general mixed blessings of servants. So while the idea of being freed from cooking or other daily tasks may initially sound appealing, you might find that supervising one or more employees may be more than you'd bargained for.

TRANSPORTATION DECISIONS
TO BUY OR NOT TO BUY A CAR, THAT IS THE QUESTION

Getting around in your new location is one of the first hurdles you'll encounter upon arrival. Local transit may be so efficient (Stockholm) or the city so crowded (Bangkok) that you wouldn't dream of driving. On the other hand, if you've moved to a small village in rural France, you may feel stranded without a car.

On each of our sabbaticals, we've chosen to have a vehicle. Usually we brought or transferred enough money to purchase a used car in good condition soon after arriving, and then sold it at the end of our stay. We even made a profit on one transaction, but that certainly was not the norm. Instead, we've generally taken quite a loss, but have tried to think of it as simply the cost of having our own wheels.

If you do decide to buy a car, here are some things to consider:

- **Parking** – Is there any? Is it free or must you pay by the month or year?
- **Gas prices** – Can you afford to drive a car once you have one?
- **Taxes and license fees** – Be sure to ask about additional expenses. For example,

England has safety inspection and annual car license fees that will add to your total costs.

- **Right-hand drive** – Depending on your destination, you may also need to consider the implications of driving on the left-hand side of the road. Approximately 50% of the world drives on the left, including the UK, Australia, New Zealand, Japan, India, China, and much of Africa. Most drivers do eventually adjust, but it's helpful to remember that "the shoulder by the window is the middle of the road." Memorize that ditty and you'll stay on the correct side *wherever* you're driving. However, don't be surprised if you find the windshield wipers flapping when you thought you'd signalled for a turn.
- **Third-world traffic** – Whether you drive on the left or right, taking to the road in a densely populated, developing country can be a nightmare. Warns author Monica Rabe (1997):

  > You might as well forget everything you have been taught about safety, courtesy and right of way… The traffic is usually congested, the air polluted, the streets often without signs and in poor condition. Many of the cars and vehicles in use would be declared dangerous in many countries. (p.57)

- **Driver's licenses** – You may be able to drive using your existing license or International Driver's License (see chapter 2, *Paperwork*). If you aren't required to take a written or driving test, you should still pick up the driver's education booklet, to become acquainted with the local traffic rules.
- **Consumer guides** – Before purchasing a new or used car, head to the library and do some research. Consulting *Choice* magazine in Australia and *Which?* in England helped us narrow our search and avoid buying a lemon.
- **Auto club membership** – Join the local automobile club at your destination or, if you're a member at home, inquire about reciprocal benefits. For example, while in Australia, we relinquished our CAA card (Canadian Automobile Association) and were given a NRMA membership (National Roads and Motoring Association). Besides emergency road service, NRMA also offered pre-purchase inspections for under $100 for new and used vehicles. If your automobile association doesn't offer this, at least arrange for a local garage to have a look at your pro-

spective purchase. Armed with that report, you may be able to negotiate a lower price or decide to give that car a miss.

- **Buy-back plan** – Some car dealers will sell you the car with the promise of buying it back at a lower set price at the end of your stay (which is fine if they're still in business when you leave).
- **Leasing** – Those who choose this option cite the advantages of getting a *new* car, no repair bills for the year, and no hassles selling it. It's worth considering if you don't mind paying more for peace of mind.
- **Buying a new car abroad** – Various automakers, such as Volvo and Peugeot in Europe, offer discounts to overseas purchasers who use the car while abroad and then ship it home. If you're in the market for a new car, this may be a good deal, but read the fine print, especially regarding taxes and import duties. You'll be in trouble if you must be out of your home country for at least one year to avoid some or all of these substantial charges, yet need to return in *under* a year's time to get a cheap airfare. Talk to local car dealers or your national automobile association for more details and advice.
- **Trade** – One year we were particularly fortunate. German friends were moving to Canada around the same time we were going to England, so we arranged to trade cars. Each vehicle was well used, so we weren't worried about new nicks and scratches. We just informally agreed to pay the operating expenses of the car we were driving, and it worked out great. While this is a rather unique situation, you might want to look into such an exchange if you can locate someone from your destination who is coming to your university.
- **"Relay selling"** – Sometimes there is a "sabbatical car" sitting in a popular destination that can be purchased and then resold to new arrivals. Such a car existed in the UK in the 1970s. Four different mathematicians from the University of Waterloo used this vehicle, selling it as one sabbatical ended and the next began. Obviously, these folks knew of each other's plans, but it might be worth advertising in your home or destination faculty's newspaper that you are looking for a vehicle. You, too, might unearth a "sabbatical car."
- **Insurance** – However you acquire your vehicle, you'll need

some sort of insurance. This is where a letter from your insurance company, describing your claims history, comes in handy. Having a clean record could save you big bucks, as most firms would likely protect themselves by setting a high premium and deductible. Even with our letter, we found huge price differences between companies. Quotes varied by as much as $400. So, phone around if you want to get the best deal.

- **Non-Car Options** – You may decide that having a car is unnecessary or too costly; or perhaps you plan to save an expensive-to-run vehicle only for longer trips. Then look into special train, bus or air passes even before you leave home. Monthly or annual discount cards and special family passes could save you a bundle, and some, such as the Eurail Pass, can only be purchased in your home country.

What about a bike? In some areas, buying a used bike could give you mobility at a very reasonable cost. Another option is purchasing new bikes and shipping them home, as one sabbatical family visiting Cambridge, England, did. Just remember that they'll figure into your luggage and customs allowances when you return.

SCHOOL DAYS

Once you've settled into your new destination, you'll need to confirm the school arrangements you made from home. If the school is expecting your child, then you can proceed with getting uniforms or other required items, and hopefully arrange a pre-enrollment visit. Your son or daughter may understandably be rather anxious about this new environment, so your enthusiasm and support will be crucial. (Of course, *your* world has also been turned upside down by this move, but since the kids will take their cue from you, try to be positive.) A play date with a classmate-to-be or a private visit with the teacher might help. While at school, ask the teacher or principal for other ideas to ease the transition. (If you didn't make educational arrangements for your children before arriving, or if your previous plans fell through, see chapter 11, *Educational Issues*, for suggestions on where to start.)

Settling in – Your child may have a number of things to adjust to: language, routine, subjects, climate, and even length of the school day. When our eldest son started kindergarten Down Under, we were surprised to learn that his class ran all day, five days a week. This schedule, plus the Aussie heat, meant that Lukas often came home and promptly fell asleep. One night, early in our stay, he even collapsed face first into his dinner! Thankfully, he soon adjusted.

Your child may also need to learn how to handle being different. As a little Canadian Down Under, Lukas encountered this whenever he opened his mouth. His peers kept asking him to "say something," so they could giggle at his accent. He took this in his stride, but being singled out can be pretty intimidating, or at least annoying, for most kids. This is particularly true if they also look different from their classmates. Normally the novelty-factor wears off in time, and by then your child will likely have developed some admirable assimilation and coping skills that will be useful in later life. If there are difficulties after the first month, though, definitely discuss this with the teacher or perhaps a school counsellor, if there is one. Since school will be your child's main social arena, it's important to nip problems in the bud.

Finding a local contact – Probably the best advice is to make every effort to connect with another parent in the class or school. Since confusing forms and notes are bound to be sent home, it's wise to have someone other than the teacher to ask. I received such a query from a Chinese couple who were living in Canada for a year. They were baffled by a letter their six-year-old brought home from school. It read: "Attached please find a list of names for Valentine's. That day is approaching very quickly." They had no idea what Valentine's Day was or why they'd been sent a list of names. So I explained that February 14th had some very specific traditions, especially in elementary schools, and described making or buying valentines for everyone in the class. I also filled them in on the more grown-up celebrations, like the exchange of candy and flowers, plus dances and romantic dinners.

In the following months, I unravelled St. Patrick's Day, April Fool's Day, and Easter as well. For the latter, I described both the religious and secular traditions, feeling rather foolish when I came to the part about rabbits that hide eggs. The couple listened politely and nodded their heads, but I wondered what they said to each other later! It's worth remembering how strange some of *our* traditions sound when you encounter seemingly bizarre rituals elsewhere.

Outside the classroom – Another important step towards easing your children's adjustment is encouraging them to participate in extracurricular activities. Sports teams, bands, computer clubs, debate teams, drama, and other special interest groups provide wonderful opportunities to get better acquainted with both teachers and students. Favorite activities from home can be continued, or brand new fields explored. Two Canadian boys discovered cricket while overseas and returned home devotees. One girl became quite proficient at netball, a sport that didn't even exist where she grew up. On the other hand, being on soccer teams for years was a plus when one boy from Canada moved to Cambridge, England. Daniel immediately fit in and was appreciated for his "football" skills. Most important, such activities offer children the chance to meet kindred spirits, others who share their passion or talent. Making friends will certainly speed your children's integration into the school and will inevitably influence their perception of the whole sabbatical.

Don't underestimate the connections that *you* can make through the school as well. One family on sabbatical in England emphasized the "absolute importance" of school on their year away. Not only did their daughters find soul mates, the parents enjoyed the camaraderie of the other mums and dads. Attending the school's endless fundraising activities allowed adult friendships to blossom easily.

Parent-teacher communication – Besides connecting with other school families, it's vitally important to speak regularly with your child's teacher. If language is a barrier, take along someone willing to translate. Regular conversations should keep small concerns from growing into problems.

Don't forget the teachers at your home school either. As you approach the end of your sabbatical, it's good to remind the principal that your child will be returning, as well as giving the teachers an idea of what's happened academically while your children have been gone. This is especially important if they will be considerably ahead or behind their classmates, because of their time away. For example, due to the difference in school calendars, our son attended the end of kindergarten and the initial six months of first grade while living in Australia. However, once home in September, he started first grade all over again. Since we'd alerted his Canadian teacher ahead of time, she arranged enrichment activities to keep his little mind going. Anything similar that you can do to smooth your child's post-sabbatical transition is worth pursuing.

Incidentally, Lukas stuck out when he returned home, too. While away he'd acquired quite an Aussie twang, which caused considerable amusement back in Canada. His accent, though, lasted precisely two weeks and then was gone (although we did manage to capture it on videotape).

HEALTH CONCERNS
AWAY FROM HOME

While I've always felt that the first two tasks in a new community were finding a church and getting a library card, globetrotting friend Julie Falkner adds one more to that list – locating an English-speaking doctor. Says Julie, "I want to know that if my husband is ill in the middle of the night, there's someone I can call."

Finding a doctor – Even if language is not an issue, you'll gain peace of mind by registering with a doctor or at least having a name to call. And Julie's right; that should be done as soon as possible. Contacts at work may be able to direct you to physicians or clinics near your home. As well, American, Canadian or British embassies often have lists of English-speaking doctors in your area. Just phone the closest office or check their websites.

In addition, you should note the local emergency number (for example, in New Zealand it's 111, not 911), as well as the location of the nearest hospital. Make sure you could find the emergency room at night if you're panicking. This is also the time to dig out the phone numbers of your hometown doctor and dentist, in case past records need to be accessed. If you had problem-free, pre-departure check-ups, you might be lucky enough to avoid seeing a dentist or doctor while you're away. But if you're like our family, on each sabbatical we've managed to have big and small medical emergencies, including a severely sprained ankle in England and a concussion in Australia. We now have hospital medical files on three continents.

Beware of the water – Apart from doctors and emergencies, you'll need to be prepared for specific local conditions. For example, if you're told, "Don't drink the water," that means avoid the ice cubes, too. Vegetables like lettuce and tomatoes will also be off limits, unless they have been rinsed in boiled water. When the local water supply is iffy, bottled water is generally available and you should even use it to brush your teeth, if you're not boiling your own water. As well, when you're out and about, choose bottled water or canned pop over local juices, just to be sure.

And what if you do drink the water by mistake? You might succumb to *Beaver Fever, Montezuma's Revenge, Delhi Belly* or *The Trots*. Whatever you call it, you'll be spending a lot of time in the bathroom. If anyone in your family does get hit with the runs, try the BRAT diet: Bananas, Rice, Applesauce, and Toast. Those four foods act as "binders" and should help get the person back to normal soon. There are also the "plug-'em-up" medicines. As my pharmacist once said, "You know that credit card ad? Forget American Express™; it's Imodium™ you shouldn't leave home without." Also, during bouts of diarrhea, watch out for dehydration problems, especially in small children. For peace of mind, carry packets of rehydration salts that you can add to safe water. If problems persist, see a doctor.

Local health precautions – If you go to tropical or very sunny locales, you'll need to protect yourself against sunburn. We encountered this when we went Down Under. Australia doesn't advertise that it's the skin cancer capital of the world, but Aussies have been heeding their Cancer Society's "slip-slop-slap" campaign for more than twenty-five years ("slip on a shirt, slop on sunscreen, and slap on a hat"). They even have skin cancer check-up vans that travel to busy beaches, so people can have their moles examined. Many school uniforms also include Legionnaires' hats (with fabric covering little necks), and classrooms provide sunscreen that kids must apply before each recess.

Bottom line, no matter where you go, ask locals what types of health precautions they observe, and follow suit. Sometimes you'll even pick up a nifty tip. While chatting with another mum on an Australian beach, I learned that she always carried a small bottle of vinegar on such outings. If her children got stung by jellyfish, she simply poured vinegar on the area, which counteracted the irritation. From then on, we were never without vinegar at the beach.

Having a baby in Holland – Of course, your health concerns could be bigger than minor jellyfish stings. You could find yourself having a baby while on sabbatical. Needless to say, this will be easier if you're in an English-speaking environment, but pregnancy and childbirth have been successfully negotiated elsewhere!

One friend had her second child while on sabbatical in Holland. Marg Paré knew she was pregnant when they left home. What she didn't know was that Holland is the homebirth center of the world (apart from places where there are no hospitals and therefore, no choice). So when Marg walked into the local medical clinic and said in stilted Dutch, "I'm pregnant. How do I find an obstetrician?" she wasn't expecting to be told where to locate the nearest midwife. It seems that almost all births in Holland are homebirths and each neighborhood has its resident practitioner.

My friend's regular pre-natal checkups were at the midwife's home, which was just a short bike ride away. Since Marg had been studying Dutch for less than a year, she was relieved to learn that her midwife could care for her in English, as well as Dutch or French. Marg also stumbled onto a prenatal aqua fit class and enjoyed connecting with other pregnant ladies. Serendipitously, some of them were fellow English-speaking expatriates.

As her due date approached, Marg had her mother mail a large box of baby things she'd packed before leaving home. The clinic also gave her a list of items to have on hand for a homebirth, including band-aids, gauze bandages, a crib, and diapers. They received this list in Dutch, as well as a bizarrely inaccurate translation in English (they actually found the Dutch list easier to understand). Then a week before she was due, the clinic loaned her "bed risers," a jack for the bed that made things more comfortable for the midwife.

When Marg went into labor (exactly when the midwife had predicted), she called and was told that two other women were already ahead of her, so the midwife might not be able to come right away. These were not comforting words, especially to her husband. In the end, the midwife arrived in time, and with her was a nurse who only spoke Dutch. This was the beginning of a few linguistic complications. At one point in the proceedings, Marg was speaking three languages – English to the midwife, Dutch to the nurse, and French with her husband. She also learned the hard way that under pressure, people always revert to their native tongue. It wasn't long before the midwife started shouting, "Push!" or "Don't push!" in Dutch. Unfortunately, Marg had always confused the words for "push" and "pull," since they're very similar. So in the heat of the moment, she wasn't sure what she was supposed to do. Eventually a little boy emerged, who was cleaned up and weighed with a portable contraption that looked like it was normally used for fish.

Since all this was happening overnight, they woke up their four-year-old, and the nurse fixed everyone a traditional Dutch, post-birth snack. Marg had been warned that she'd need special buns and pink anise sprinkles on hand, but she hadn't expected the nurse to turn hostess. In fact, this would continue to be the nurse's role for the following week. Her job description not only included assisting at the birth, but spending each day at Marg's home. Her title in Dutch actually meant "the nurse who comes to stay after your baby is born." She was there to help care for the new baby, cook meals, run errands, buy groceries, do laundry, babysit older siblings, escort children to school, and even receive guests and serve tea and cookies! In Holland, everyone visits the new parents and baby during that first week, so having a built-in hostess makes a lot of sense.

The services of a specialized nurse for seven days were part of the "package deal" that included the midwife's pre-natal care and the homebirth. This package is free for the Dutch, but Marg had to pay for the actual delivery. She felt it was an excellent system and would definitely have a baby there again. Although initially unnerved by the prospect of giving birth at home, she now thinks the process, especially the postpartum care, is much better than in North America.

And what about citizenship? Being born in Holland did not make the Paré's son Dutch. Instead, the parents had to race around to various offices and embassies to register their son's birth and obtain the necessary papers, so that they could legally fly home together. But that seemed like a small price to pay for such a special souvenir of their sabbatical.

Keeping in Touch
with Home

Thank goodness for advances in communications! Whether you're a neo-Luddite or a computer geek, while on sabbatical you'll reap the benefits of the technological breakthroughs of the past decades. Staying in touch with friends and loved ones has never been easier or cheaper.

Telephones – One Canadian friend remembers overseas calls being so expensive on their first sabbatical that they limited themselves to one per month. Between phone calls they waited anxiously for letters. Thirty years later they could phone home from New Zealand for only seventeen cents a minute, and did so frequently. Today it's even less.

Soon after arriving, you should check out long-distance options, particularly pre-paid, long-distance phone cards for specific countries. Don't just talk to your phone company; quiz other long-term visitors about their telephone choices. You might also investigate the cost of using calling cards from your home phone company, or see if it's cheaper for friends and relatives to call you. This is another area where diligent detective work pays off.

Email – Speedy and inexpensive, email is the natural choice for keeping in touch with friends and family while on sabbatical. It's also a particularly efficient means for tenants to contact you with questions or concerns. As well, email bypasses that pesky problem of time zones. (You'll appreciate this if you've ever received a phone call at 4 a.m. because someone miscalculated the time difference.) Another benefit is that, if you print your emails or simply save your files, you can painlessly generate a journal at the same time. Reluctant journal keepers (you or your children) might be more willing to write friends than scribble in an empty book, thus killing two birds with one stone.

Some families prefer sending regular, mass email newsletters to stay in touch. This can be a time-saver, but first consider if everyone on your list really *wants* to hear all those details. (I'm reminded of a story about a child who asked her school librarian for a book about penguins. The librarian happily found such a book and checked it out for her. A week later, the girl returned the volume and the librarian asked if she'd liked it. "Yes," came the reply, "but it told me more about penguins than I wanted to know.") Remember that when writing your group epistles.

Of course, younger family members may consider email passé. They likely already have accounts on Facebook or other social networking sites and will easily remain connected with friends, no matter where they're living.

Homepages – Another possibility is setting up your own website or blog, complete with photos, video clips, and commentary. This can be a family project or the special responsibility of just one child. In this way, only those who are interested will visit your site, and computer-savvy grandparents can enjoy regular updates on the grandkids.

Cameras and microphones – Small webcams attached to your computer as well as your correspondent's will allow you even more interaction. Or if you'd like to visit sight unseen, investigate Internet telephony software using microphones at each end, such as Skype. (See *Resources* for details.)

Video – If you can film your kids lining up at their new school and meeting the local wildlife, you can share those special moments with friends and family back home. We have great footage of our children cuddling a koala and playing on Aussie beaches, waves crashing in the background. Posting video clips like these really helps reduce the distance, and years later you'll enjoy watching them as well.

Snail mail – Some people prefer receiving letters and postcards, even if they regularly use the Internet. One friend specifically requested that I send her a *real* postcard with a *real* stamp. In addition to postcards, I generally send a family newsletter midway through our time, just to keep people informed of our activities, and to let them know they're not forgotten. Snail mail also allows you to enclose photos and grandparent-pleasing children's drawings.

You've got mail – It's great to get news from home, so be sure that you liberally distribute your sabbatical snail and email addresses. Receiving such mailings can be bittersweet, though. One year a neighbor wrote that the daffodils in my front yard were lovely, prompting a minor bout of homesickness. Thoughtful friends have also included clippings from our local paper.

Some families subscribe to newsmagazines from home or read news online, in order to stay on top of cultural and political events. We, on the other hand, revelled in reading international newspapers and magazines, enjoying the different perspectives.

So whether your communications are high-tech or via pigeon post, set aside time to nurture those relationships you've left behind. Not only will the recipients be delighted, you'll reap the benefits when you return. You won't feel like Rip van Winkle, unaware of what has happened in your absence, and your friends and relatives will have gained some insights into your sabbatical life.

LANGUAGE LEARNING ABROAD

If you've settled in a country where English is not the first language, it's time to knuckle down and learn those verbs! Whatever you managed to study prior to departure will come in handy now, but expect to be overwhelmed. Signs, clerks, and forms all seem to conspire against you. A simple request or purchase becomes a major ordeal. There's an obvious solution: you need more language proficiency.

Pedagogical options – The suggestions in chapter 12 still stand; intensive or weekly classes, tutors, books, CDs, computer software, and online courses are all possibilities. Ask local contacts, especially other expats, for recommendations.

Where you live can even provide a true immersion experience. Shirley and Jay Thomson said the best thing that happened to them on their sabbatical in Sweden, linguistically or otherwise, was renting a house in the middle of a Stockholm suburb. While their friendly neighbors spoke English and wanted to practice, the couple needed a functional level of Swedish to interact with shopkeepers and the tradespeople who fixed their appliances. They also wanted to participate in social events in the neighborhood, where conversations were entirely in Swedish. So they threw themselves into language lessons, and while they never became fluent, their increasing comprehension allowed them to have animated exchanges. In one case, Shirley even carried on an enjoyable, bilingual friendship with someone who spoke to her only in Swedish, while she responded in English. They each found it easier to express their deeper thoughts and feelings in their native tongue, but had enough knowledge to understand the other's language.

Young children seem to respond especially well to immersion, since there's no better incentive to learning a language than a desire to play and communicate with other kids. When one little girl moved to Holland, she started kindergarten, and by the end of the week she was chattering away in Dutch. Your kids will likely master the foreign language faster than you will, so swallow your pride and learn from the littlest. They will also happily correct your pronunciation, which is, admittedly, a mixed blessing.

There are also many easy, inexpensive things you can do at home. I've used 3" x 5" cards with nouns written on them (words for chair, lamp, table, etc.) and plastered them on the appropriate items around the house. I also studied anything that came in the door, including cereal boxes and toothpaste tubes. Attempting to read the local newspaper is an excellent habit as well. (Don't underestimate the sheer glee of understanding a headline!) Take a look at the ads and obituaries, too. You'll be surprised by what you are soon able to assimilate.

While we rarely watch television at home, overseas it is a remarkably effective tutor. One family on sabbatical in Holland religiously tuned in the Dutch version of *Sesame Street*. While this was ostensibly for their four-year-old, the parents' vocabulary grew painlessly as well. Even if you're fluent in the native tongue, television will provide innumerable insights into your new location. Watch the nightly news and notice the order of the headlines and the reporters' pronunciation. Pay attention to the commercials, too – they may teach you more than the news! In addition, vegging in front of the TV soon after arrival is a great way to let your travel-whacked family relax and connect with the new culture.

Another fun teaching method is borrowing or buying children's books, especially volumes you already know and love. (I collect *Winnie-the-Pooh* in various languages; you should see it in Thai!) However, novices can probably improve their vocabulary best by seeking out toddler books, children's dictionaries, and beginning readers.

Julie Falkner, a New Zealand friend who studied French intensively after moving to Montreal, observed that

> ...sometimes learning a new word is as easy as noticing a title in a bookstore: *Jonathan Livingston le goéland*. The TV Guide can also be useful; having learnt that a *naufragé* is a shipwrecked person, I was pleased to discover a programme called *Les Joyeux Naufragés*. [Husband] Miguel laughed as he explained that I'd stumbled on a French version of *Gilligan's Island!*

Be careful what you learn – Monica Rabe (1997) warns, "It seems sometimes to be easier to swear in a foreign language because the words do not carry the emotional charge that swear words do in your native language. However, they might offend the persons to whom you are talking" (p. 67).

I witnessed this while chatting with a Chinese friend who was studying in Canada. Since Philip's English was very good, I was surprised when he started inserting rather potent swear words into our conversation. So I asked him if he normally swore in China, and he said, "No." It turned out that he'd picked up this advanced vocabulary from his Canadian roommates and had no idea how foul-mouthed he sounded. He thanked me profusely and credited me with saving him from future embarrassment, especially in front of his professors.

Despite this potential problem, acquiring local words and expressions can be an enjoyable part of your sabbatical. While we could never sound like native Australians, our family quickly incorporated a number of terms into our daily conversation, such as *uni* for university, *mozzie* for mosquito, and *nappies* for diapers. The latter term was adopted soon after arrival because I tired of being teased every time I said I was going to change my son's diaper. It was just easier to go native. Incidentally, some of these Aussie words are still embedded in our family's lexicon, even though many years have passed.

Conversational confusion – Sometimes technology can magnify, rather than simplify communication problems. While living in Switzerland, my husband and I tried to avoid answering the phone, shouting "YOU get it!" each time it rang. Since there were no visual cues to follow, we came to dread telephone conversations. Friends were no problem, as they knew to speak slowly. It was the window washers, carpet cleaners, and other telemarketers who sent us running for cover. Eventually we learned to say, "I'm sorry, I don't understand" in stilted German, and then we just hung up.

You may also find yourself floundering in a country where you *thought* you spoke the same language. While you can look up new words, you're on your own when coping with accents. For instance, when a friend was given directions to a building at Queensland University, the Aussie instructions sounded like *Dye Block*. After unsuccessfully searching the campus, she finally realized that some of the buildings were lettered and that she was actually looking for *D* Block.

My own worst case of accent anxiety occurred on our first sabbatical in London. I stopped the neighborhood milkman and asked what the cost would be for regular delivery. I was absolutely flummoxed by the East End flavoring of his words and asked him to repeat the information three times. Unfortunately, I still didn't have a clue about the arrangements or price, so I decided that the easiest course of action was to thank him and say I wasn't interested. Politeness (and cowardice) won out.

When all else fails – I once knew a student who was staying in a chilly, Russian hotel with inadequate bedding. While her friends attempted to assemble a grammatically correct request for additional blankets, she just flopped down on the floor and pretended to be cold, producing immediate results from the staff.

If pantomime isn't your style, consider buying one of the "point to it" books. These ingenious booklets could be a lifesaver when your linguistic skills fail. I have one that is filled with a cornucopia of color photos (and no words). You simply point to what you want or are asking about ("toilet?" "towel?") and the local person responds by nodding or pointing to another photo. It's a fascinating and very handy reference. (See *Resources* for details.)

VISITORS
OR HOW NOT TO FEEL LIKE A HOTEL

If you go to an enticing location, friends and relatives will fol-low. This is usually a mixed blessing. While you're delighted to share your new surroundings with special friends and family members, you didn't move here to open a hotel. One friend la-mented that so many people visited them during their year away that they barely had time to do things just as a family.

Practical considerations – Of course, there are also logistical issues. Do you have the space for guests? Do you have enough towels and bedding? If you've lived in an area long enough, you may have friends who would lend you spare linen for the dura-tion. On the other hand, you could follow the lead of the Millerd family – all visitors were requested to bring their own sheets and towels, and those coming from the Millerd's hometown were told that they could only bring one piece of luggage with them, as they would be returning with an extra box or suitcase. Guests who accepted these conditions were then welcomed with open arms.

Setting boundaries and holidaying with your guests – If that doesn't stem the tide of visitors, try blacking out periods for your holidays and letting people know that those dates simply aren't available. Alternatively, you could travel *with* your visitors, e.g., renting a larger holiday cottage and sharing the costs. We found this to be an enjoyable way to have our vacations and entertain guests, too. The point is to think about it ahead of time, so you don't become a (hotel) doormat.

Outings

One of the joys of sabbatical life is increased family time, both in quantity and quality. Your weekends suddenly become your own. Yard work, house repairs, and other projects are likely someone else's problems. Work pressures tend to subside. (At home my husband routinely went back to the university on the weekends, while on sabbatical his projects seemed to confine themselves to Monday to Friday.) Committee meetings and other volunteer commitments are probably fewer, as are your children's invitations to birthday parties. In short, you've been given the gift of time.

With the calendar clear, it's possible to take off on weekend explorations and longer holidays. In fact, it's not unusual for families to disappear almost every weekend while on sabbatical. Here are some suggestions to make the most of this opportunity:

Solicit advice – While guidebooks are helpful, nothing beats word-of-mouth recommendations. Ask locals about their favorite daytrips or vacation destinations. Find out where they take their out-of-town guests. Pick the brains of fellow visitors, too. They'll understand your time constraints and the need to "see it all now." In fact, locals are often amazed by how much sightseeing sabbatical families can cram into their short time, doing more in a year than the natives may in a lifetime!

Look into family memberships – The Harpers purchased a National Trust membership while in England and felt it was the best money they'd spent all year. They visited wonderfully preserved houses and attended special events all over the country, making history come alive for their four daughters. During our time in Oxford, we splurged and also bought a National Trust membership, as well as ones for English Heritage and the National Art Collections Fund. Between these three organizations, we were able to see just about everything we wanted in the UK for "free." So while we laid out the initial, daunting sum of $350, we paid no further entrance fees to enjoy their properties or programs during the year. As members, we also received discounts, newsletters, maps, and handy guidebooks. Best of all, we spontaneously visited sites we hadn't expected to, and were able to return to our favorites without weighing the cost.

You might also consider joining a hostel organization, such as the International Youth Hostel Federation, also known as Hostelling International (HI). Most of these establishments offer family rooms and will likely save you money over competing accommodations. However, large families should beware. When the Harpers' tent blew away while camping in Cornwall, England, they decided to stay in a local hostel. To their chagrin, they learned that they and their four children didn't qualify as a family, but were considered a "small colony" and were charged accordingly.

Keep the troops happy en route – Once you've chosen your destination, do all you can to ensure you have happy travellers. Music, books, toys – whatever it takes, pack it! When our children were young, I followed the same routine on the ground as I had in the air, wrapping small books and toys and distributing them strategically during the trip. The kids couldn't wait for these surprises, and happily settled down *most* of the time. Teens and toddlers particularly appreciate having their own music. However, if you can't abide Top 40 or Barney, consider investing in personal CD or MP3 players. Just be sure that the kids have their own backpacks to carry all this gear. They should take responsibility for their own belongings by the time they're four. A good rule of thumb, if you can think in metric, is that kids can "walk their age and carry half of it," e.g., a twelve-year-old can walk 12 km/day and carry a pack weighing 6 kg (Lanigan, 2002, p. 24).

Don't forget food and drinks. Water bottles instead of pop will reduce the problems associated with spills, but be prepared for numerous pit stops. You can also save time and money by packing lunches. Brown-bagging has allowed us to enjoy some memorable al fresco meals in fabulous locations – on the banks of London's Thames River across from St. Paul's cathedral, in the middle of a "Heidi meadow" in the Swiss Alps, and on stunning

Aussie beaches. A Frisbee™ or soccer ball is also useful to "shake the sillies out" at rest stops.

For more ideas on travelling with children, check out Vicki Lansky's *Trouble-Free Travel with Children*, Cathy Lanigan's *Travel with Children*, and the Portnoys' *How to Take Great Trips with Your Kids*. (See *Resources* for details.)

Process what they see – Some of what your family encounters during your travels will be difficult to cope with, such as beggars, abject poverty, open sewers, and dead animals hanging in markets. If possible, talk to your children ahead of time about the sights, sounds, and particularly smells that might overwhelm them. Depending on their age, you may want to discuss the shortage of affordable housing, or you might decide to carry an apple to give the homeless man on the corner when you go out. Debrief your children's reactions and concerns, and perhaps investigate ways you can help.

Keeping a journal will crystallize their impressions. If you're lucky, your children will jump at the chance to scribble their thoughts in a diary. If not, try prodding daily entries by asking them to list new foods they've tried (giving one to five stars for taste), noting things that seem different from home or what they particularly like, and collecting new words and expressions, not necessarily in another language. (Our Australian list included *barbie, ute,* and *bonzer*.) Non-writers can draw what they see, so can older children. This journal/diary could easily evolve into a scrapbook with the addition of postcards, stamps, candy wrappers, and even labels from juice bottles. Not only is a journal a great way to process experiences, it could become one of their favorite souvenirs.

Plan kid-friendly activities – Unless your sabbatical is in the middle of Antarctica, you'll probably want to include some museums and other cultural or educational destinations in your itinerary. If so, it might be worth remembering Nancy S. Messner's (1991) astute observation: "Museums generate in the young boredom, curiosity, embarrassing questions and interest – in that order" (p. 52).

To minimize the potential boredom, plan ahead: visit when the kids are fresh; avoid long lines; don't try to see everything; and trade off time spent in museums, art galleries, and cathedrals with kids' activities like playgrounds, zoos, children's museums, and amusement parks. Another tactic is to send one parent off with the kids to a nearby playground when they get rangy, freeing the other parent to continue browsing the exhibits. Of course, if you really want to sightsee without children, consider hiring a babysitter for part of a day, or even taking one with you. Hotels can often provide referrals.

Most of all, you'll need to reduce your expectations and acknowledge that you won't see the displays the same way you would *sans enfants*. Indeed, you'll have more success if you think like a kid. According to Sanford and Joan Portnoy (1995), "Favorite activities for children on any kind of trip often involve 1) heights, 2) water, 3) unusual modes of transportation, 4) animals, or 5) any combination of these" (p. 25). I'd add food to that list, especially from buffets or street vendors, but if you keep these suggestions in mind, you won't go wrong.

I have my own theory about what really interests kids, though – activities they can *do*, not just *watch*. Our children were eight and twelve when we were on sabbatical in Oxford, and we planned outings for almost every weekend, plus several trips in Europe.

Heights are a hit.

A few months after returning to Canada, I asked the boys to list the highlights of their year away. The first thing mentioned was trying glassblowing in Denmark. They also liked England's Kenilworth Castle ruins where they attacked each other with imaginary swords. Windsor's Legoland was a big hit, of course, but so was hiking in the Swiss Alps and cross-country skiing in Lapland. In addition, two of their other top memories were watching *Match of the Day*, the BBC's weekly soccer highlights, and visiting Blackwell's, their favorite bookstore in Oxford.

If there's a theme here, it's probably that most of these activities involved *doing* something. If you aim to follow your children's interests and keep them active, you'll have happier campers. Yet sometimes even an outing you're sure they'll enjoy flops. Who knows why; maybe they're tired, grumpy or simply museumed-out. When that happens, just follow the advice of one wise dad and buy the kids an ice cream and buy yourself a beer!

How to Handle the Holidays

Being away from home and family during holidays produces mixed emotions. You are particularly aware of how distant you are, of whom and what you're missing, and of those who are missing you. It's not unusual to feel sadness, homesickness or even guilt. On the other hand, you are suddenly free from traditions and family expectations and can do what you really would like to do, possibly for the first time in your life. If you embrace holidays as wonderful opportunities rather than difficult periods simply to endure, you may wistfully look back on these celebrations for many years to come.

National holidays (yours and theirs) – Packing a small flag is a good idea for a number of reasons. It can be on display at home, taken to school for show-and-tell, or used to celebrate your country's birthday. Each year on the 4th of July, you'll find the stars and stripes on view as Americans around the world gather for celebratory picnics and parties. Sometimes the local consulate or embassy will organize special activities, or you could arrange one yourself.

The Harper family used Canada Day (July 1st) to host a party. Since their year in Oxford was drawing to a close, they planned a picnic to say thank you and goodbye to their new friends, and to highlight their national holiday.

In Switzerland we enjoyed celebrating National Day on August 1st with the rest of the village where we lived. We joined the torchlight parade as it wound its way out to a field. Traditional costumes were worn and the crowd sang with gusto. We couldn't follow much of the speeches, as they were in the local dialect, but it was great fun participating in something that our neighbors so obviously enjoyed. Long before the party was over, we walked home, where our elderly landladies had decorated our farmhouse with a string of red and white Swiss flags.

Canadian Thanksgiving – On our first sabbatical, we lived in international housing in central London. When I learned that the cafeteria planned an annual turkey dinner to celebrate American Thanksgiving in November, but not Canadian Thanksgiving, I pointed out the oversight to the powers-that-be. Then I got the names of all the Canadians in the complex and arranged for us to share a turkey dinner together on the second Monday in October. The staff had been unaware that this holiday was observed on a different day in Canada, but they were happy to accommodate us. I even rustled up a Canadian flag for the occasion!

Easter – We've been fortunate to celebrate Easter Sunday in many places around the world, including a sunrise service on an Aussie beach with the waves pounding in the background. But without doubt, our most unusual Easter was spent at a Finnish Orthodox monastery near the Russian border. While we were on sabbatical in Switzerland, Finnish friends invited us to join them on their annual retreat. The candles, incense, icons, and singing provided a unique perspective on this holy day.

Christmas – Worship services were also an important component of our Christmas celebrations, but this holiday, perhaps more than any other, carries with it an enormous amount of cultural baggage. Your children may feel that certain traditions *must* be included or they may have some imaginative alternatives of their own.

When the MacKay family was on sabbatical in New Zealand, their school-age daughters insisted they would not have a Christmas tree because, since it *couldn't* be like home, they didn't want to even try. Instead, the girls decorated the house with paper chains and popcorn strings they'd made, and secretly worked on clues for hidden presents. On Christmas Eve they wrote names on plastic grocery bags for stockings, and hung them on the staircase. Family members then filled the "stockings" with only consumable gifts, things that could be used up or eaten before they returned home seven months later. This rule, while prompted by concern over packing limitations, produced some very creative ideas. The girls gave their father a bottle of wine and their mother some stationery, while the parents gave each of their daughters one "free" telephone call, so they could chat with a friend back home.

While one family I spoke with always packed a few Christmas decorations when going on sabbatical, I never included any holiday-related items except Christmas music. Instead, we borrowed pre-loved trees from friends and made our own decorations. Some of these continue to elicit fond memories years later, especially the homemade ornaments of seashells and sparkly yarn. I also bought or borrowed candles, since they really made things cozy on dark winter nights.

On the other hand, celebrating Christmas Down Under meant summer and heat, a change that we relished. On Christmas morning, while most Aussies were still at home opening presents, we headed straight for the beach. Not surprisingly, we met a family there who had emigrated from Scotland and who said that they came to the beach every year, just so they could tell their Scottish relatives on the phone later that day! So rather than missing a "White Christmas," savvy expatriates revel in the differences.

THE PROBLEM
SABBATICAL

Some sabbaticals are memorable for all the wrong reasons. Instead of soaring like eagles, they sputter and careen into walls. The problems may be due to poor planning, health concerns, dreary accommodations, lousy climate, hassles at school, professional disillusionment or all of the above. Whatever the reason, when faced with such circumstances, families have to make a decision – stay and cope with the difficulties or just cut their losses and head home.

When it's not all roses – One family looks back on their time in England with frustration and disappointment. They had planned to spend a year there, thinking that the experience would be similar to a previous sabbatical they had enjoyed at an American university. Unfortunately, they did not find the academic environment they had hoped for. The person with whom the husband had planned to work left the college soon after they arrived, and research opportunities and seminars were dismal. In hindsight, they felt they should have asked a lot more questions and investigated the department more closely before choosing it as a sabbatical destination.

There were other complications, too. His wife was trying to complete her Ph.D. thesis, and found it harder to access necessary research material than she'd expected. Making friends was more difficult, too. She emphasized that these concerns regarding her research and their social life would not, of themselves, have prompted them to abandon ship; they just compounded the academic problems. After three months, they seriously discussed heading home, but in the end, they decided to stay because it was not financially feasible to leave. They had signed a lease in the U.K., their house in Canada was rented for a year, plus there would be complications regarding their children's schooling. Faced with these realities, the family chose to soldier on. While they admitted that things never really got better, they believed that "when life hands you lemons, you make lemonade." So they made the best of things, travelling and playing tourist in their spare time. They did shorten their stay, though, heading home two months early.

It is interesting that their children, while also keen to return prematurely, had flourished in the local school, and had especially enjoyed the extracurricular activities. Their teen-aged daughter even flew back to England to visit a friend the following year. So while the sabbatical was a major disappointment for the family, it was not a complete loss.

During those initial months, it's often hard to tell if you're just suffering from the settling-in blues, or something more. When Sharon Kalbfleisch recalled their sabbatical in London, she remembers feeling completely overwhelmed. Not only was it their first time living abroad, they were also first-time parents with no support system. Their flat had a tiny fridge, so she always seemed to be shopping (with baby). There was no washer or dryer, so she was constantly heading to the laundromat (with baby). In fact, she seemed to be perpetually pushing a pram, and felt increasingly isolated and lonely. Eventually, she found a way out of her dilemma by getting a job and hiring a nanny.

However, during a subsequent sabbatical in Belgium, the Kalbfleisch's baby-related complications prompted a different decision. When Sharon was pregnant for the second time, she learned that she was expecting twins. Language barriers made discussions about everything from indigestion to ultrasound results tedious or impossible. This, plus concerns about the pregnancy, led them to cut short their sojourn and head home.

Staying and coping – Health issues also affected the quality of the MacKays' sabbatical in New Zealand. As keen naturalists and bird watchers, Jock and Samm had looked forward to extensive hiking during their time abroad. Unfortunately, Samm was laid low by a knee injury early in their sabbatical. This forced them to curtail or abort many of their plans, and colored their entire time away. It's worth noting, though, that the MacKays, as well as the previously mentioned families, all went on subsequent sabbaticals.

Then there were the Wilsons in Washington, D.C. Recounts Anne,

> ...Tom took a sabbatical at the University of Maryland. What a year that was! The rented house was a horror show; the interior was black and gray, the basement was frequently flooding, and the clothes dryer sparked flames. Summer in D.C. is hot and humid – we had one air conditioner. The school was a disappointment to the children academically and socially. And health problems plagued us. (Huss, 2002, p. 96)

Despite this, they stuck it out and can even laugh about it now. In fact, they consider that year a wonderful family time. So don't be depressed or dissuaded by these tales of woe. The message is clear, "It's still worth it!"

HEADING BACK HOME

Turning Your Face Toward Home
The Six-Weeks-Till-Departure Phenomenon

If the sabbatical has been a positive experience, you'll likely have been so preoccupied with day-to-day life and travel that thoughts of home will have been rather fleeting. Nevertheless, there comes a point where the balance is tipped on an invisible scale and suddenly you are in the home stretch.

It happened for us on our Oxford sabbatical after the final set of overseas visitors left. That was in mid-July, six weeks before our departure. Conversations became increasingly sprinkled with references to our house, school, and stores in Canada, and (this was key) what foods we'd eat as soon as we got back. (Hamburgers were on top of our kids' list, since we'd been avoiding British beef after the Mad Cow Disease scare.)

The countdown begins – Crossing things off our Places To Visit/Things To Do list became a high priority, since I wanted to leave with as few regrets as possible. Towards that end, we made four daytrips to London in ten days, which was exhausting, but worthwhile. I also began scheduling those final dinners with friends and penultimate play dates for the kids.

Another sure sign of our impending departure was my preoccupation with purchasing "goodbye gifts" for local friends and we-thought-of-you-while-we-were-gone presents to lug back home. My husband couldn't understand why I spent so much time brooding over the right gift and then even more time tracking it down. (We have this same discussion when *not* on sabbatical; it's just that suddenly exchange rates, customs allowances, and baggage weight limits entered the picture.)

Countdown lists proved helpful. On separate sheets I prioritized what had to be done on the final day, on the three or four days before departure, in the two weeks prior to that, and finally what could be done even further ahead. The latter included delivering gifts to friends, returning all books to the library, and lots of tasks related to cleaning the house, including deciding what to do with the garbage on the last day. Having those lists before me for a month helped focus my efforts when I wasn't feeling the pressure (or desire) to clean, sort, and pack. But I knew from hard experience just how horrid life gets when it all has to be done NOW, and you end up locking the door and turning over the keys while continuing to pack in the driveway. (Don't laugh; it happened to us in Australia.)

Disconnecting – With just over a month left of the sabbatical, we reluctantly admitted that our time was limited, and began to disconnect from the place where we had become so rooted. This can be a rather emotional experience, especially if you've made good friends and fallen in love with your adopted home. I clearly remember standing in our kitchen in Oxford lamenting, "I don't *want* to go! Couldn't we just stay six more months?" Unfortunately, remaining wasn't an option, so I had to concentrate on tying up the ends of our sabbatical life.

The boys, too, were becoming more focused on "back home." They had certain purchases they wanted to make for themselves and others before leaving, and began emailing their friends with our arrival information. Not surprisingly, they soon received invitations to come and play, and our post-arrival calendar began to fill up. Our sabbatical was coming to an end.

Pre-departure Panic

As I lurched between sadness and anticipation during those last weeks, I was continually shocked by the cold reality of all that had to be done. It's one thing to "turn" toward home; it's another to actually get in the car or on the plane. Unfortunately, there's an enormous amount of angst and elbow grease in between.

First things first – You'll need to get your paperwork in order. If you are flying, your ticket requires a correct return date. Some airlines won't issue tickets with your "real" date listed, because they book only 330 days ahead. You then have to contact them closer to your planned return to have it adjusted, probably incurring a penalty in the process. (This should have been made clear when you purchased the tickets.) Alternatively, your plans may have changed (nothing like a coup in Fiji to shift stopovers), or you've simply decided to leave earlier or later than originally scheduled.

If you're lucky, these adjustments will be smooth and you'll soon have your new tickets and itinerary in hand. If not, badger the airline until you are reasonably satisfied. You may find you cannot fly home when you would like or your stopover may no longer be possible. The real stress-inducer is learning that your airline is about to go under or your tickets have been cancelled. Breathe deeply and call, fax or email your travel agent back home, if you can't get satisfaction from the local airline representative. Whatever it takes, get these matters settled as soon as possible, since your departure date acts as the catalyst for the final weeks.

If you haven't done so already, send a note (a scenic postcard is nice) to your family doctor and dentist, requesting appointments for everyone in the month following your arrival. It's also a good idea to remind the principal at your school back home that your children will be returning.

Selling the car – With your return date set, you're ready to tackle bigger challenges. If you purchased a vehicle without a buy-back agreement, you need to unload it. Although you'll likely want to keep the car as long as possible, selling is such a hassle you should make that your first priority.

Advertise everywhere – university and grocery store bulletin boards, church newsletters, the local paper, and especially auto trader publications. Blatantly tell everyone you know that you have a great car to sell. Print up ads and hand them out. One year our estate agent even offered to email a notice throughout his company, so that other agents dealing with in-coming customers could be alerted. Leave no stone unturned!

At the end of our Oxford sabbatical, despite all our efforts, the response was still pathetic. We'd only had two inquiries, and one of them just wanted to know the car's color. The other individual initially agreed to buy it, but then pulled out. Since that happened only weeks before leaving, panic began to set in. (We later learned that August is simply a lousy month to sell a car in Oxford, because most new visitors don't arrive until mid-to-late September.) In the end we left our car with a friend in Cambridge, who eventually decided to buy it himself. It's times like these that "buy-back arrangements" and "car leasing" sound mighty appealing!

But this was nothing compared to what our friends went through. The Harpers were still trying to sell their English car within an hour of leaving. The night before their departure, Mark had arranged to meet a prospective buyer in a local pub. Due to Mark's anxiety about selling it quickly, this fellow was suspicious and thought the car was "hot." So he and another friend talked with Mark, then left the pub. Soon after a police officer walked in, went straight to Mark, and began questioning him about his car. Once Mark proved that he owned the vehicle and explained the reason for his urgency, the bobby said *he* knew someone who might be interested! Unfortunately, that lead was also a dead end.

The next morning the Harpers still had the aging station wagon to sell, as well as an 11:30 a.m. bus to catch. So Mark visited the owner of a car dealership around the corner who had once expressed interest, but had made a ridiculously low offer. Nothing looked ridiculous anymore! Without letting on that his family was about to leave the country, Mark praised the car, but mentioned that the clutch was having problems. For that reason, he said, he'd consider reducing his asking price. The car salesman suggested a figure, Mark said, "Sold!," took the check, and sprinted to meet his family. He gave his wife a thumbs-up, grabbed the luggage, waved to the neighbors who were gathered to say goodbye, and then finally joined the line for the bus to the airport.

How much can you shove in? – If selling your car isn't nerve-wracking enough, then try getting all of your belongings back into your suitcases. If you're like us, you'll have accumulated a few purchases along the way. My weakness is books, which unfortunately wreak havoc with luggage weight restrictions. One year we reduced this problem by sending boxes back with visitors from our hometown. We used rope to fashion handles, and made sure we packed these makeshift suitcases in front of our guests, so they could honestly say they knew what was inside. We also provided complete customs information for them, including prices. It was a great way to get rid of winter clothes that were no longer needed and some of the flotsam and jetsam of our travels.

Of course, if you're flying and are wildly over the maximum weight, you have a problem. In this case, you can: 1) check extra luggage and pay the stiff excess baggage fee, *if* the airline will let the bags on; 2) investigate shipping boxes home, either by sea or air, also not cheap; 3) sweet talk your way through check-in without a penalty, as one family successfully did (exclaiming over the wonderful year they'd just spent in the country and how they were now on their way home), but be prepared to be met with a smile and a firm request for funds; or 4) use the triage method: abandon the heaviest items, wear as many of your clothes as possible, and shove heavy things in your pockets and carry-on bags. You still may get hit with a charge, but it won't be as high. Beware, though; these fees may need to be paid in the local currency, not with credit cards.

Desperation cleaning – Even when your departure is booked, the car is sold, and most of the packing is done, you still have to clean the house or apartment you've rented. I must confess I hate this task and procrastinate as long as possible. Yet on one sabbatical, I had a flash of inspiration. Friends had given us chocolates as a goodbye gift and there was an unfinished bottle of sherry in the cupboard. Since I obviously didn't want to pack these items, I decided we should indulge. So, on the night we'd set aside for tackling the kitchen, I stuffed myself with chocolates while my husband toasted me with sherry, and I must say I've never enjoyed cleaning a kitchen more!

Goin' home – You should pamper yourself on the actual trip, too. After a frazzled departure (is there any other kind?), treat yourself to a nice meal, a novel you've been meaning to read, or a relaxing, mid-trip shower in an airport transit lounge (the best four dollars I've ever spent!). There will be enough upheaval when you arrive home; enjoy being in limbo while you can.

WHAT CONDITION IS THE HOUSE IN?

Many returnees approach their home with trepidation. How will it look? What will be missing or broken? How much time, energy, and money will need to be invested to put things right? It is particularly disheartening to face appliance repairs, cleaning, and painting after you've just scoured and scrubbed your sabbatical residence. Yet rarely do people cross the threshold and find everything in the same condition as they left it. At such times it might help to remember that if *your* family had lived in the house for the past year, things wouldn't look exactly the same either.

Sometimes the problems are fairly minor. One family returned home to find some of their tenants' toys and videos scattered around the house. As well, a piece of trim had been pulled off the fireplace, there was water damage on the teak furniture, and strangely, none of the telephones worked. The tenants had also used oven cleaner on the self-cleaning oven, but the owners figured they'd gotten off lightly.

Hassles and horror stories – Truly irresponsible tenants cause far greater headaches. In one case, the tenant had not regularly paid his rent and the homeowners had already had to chase down checks while on sabbatical. Then upon returning, they were informed of an unreported break-in. The television was gone, and the owners later noted other items that were missing. While the landlords were suspicious, they didn't feel able to pursue the matter.

When another family returned home from their sabbatical, they were shocked to find that the three female students who had rented their home had completely ignored the stipulations of the lease. The owners had offered the students a reduced rent on the condition they would not sublet during the summer. But they learned from their neighbors that five male students, plus one female, had lived there during the previous four months. In addition, the tenants abandoned a TV, numerous beds, and assorted furniture, and left rotting food in the fridge. As well, it looked as though no one had ever touched a sponge or broom. The bathroom was so disgusting the family took a photograph for posterity, flabbergasted that anyone could live in such squalor.

Even if your home is just visited or occasionally lived in by relatives, you may still be unpleasantly surprised. One couple's car had a dead battery, which delayed the initial grocery run, as well as other essential errands. The sink in the upstairs bathroom was clogged, and when the plumber came, he had to bash a hole in the bedroom wall to gain access to the pipe. Even more aggravating, the water heater had broken, so there was no hot water for showers to wash away the accumulated grime of thirty-six hours spent flying home.

Appliance death (or appliance non-compliance) seems to be a common occurrence after returning from sabbatical. Our water softener was leaking and needed to be replaced one year, and another time our washing machine was on the blink. Again, these repairs and replacements might have been required if we'd been living in the house, but it's discouraging (and expensive) to face them immediately upon arrival. Alison Morrison pragmatically addressed this issue on her (now defunct) *Sensational Sabbatical Suggestions* website:

> The key is to expect that when you come back to your house it will be in worse condition than when you left. No matter what you do to prevent this, it happens. Plan to come home and spend weeks fixing up the home and yard, and to spend several hundreds of dollars to replace and repair things. If this bothers you, build it into the rent you plan to charge or do not rent it out.

Holding your possessions lightly – Basically, you'll need to relax your grip on your belongings, if you're going to leave them in someone else's care. After our first sabbatical, we found the expected leftover food, ashes in the fireplace, and uncleaned fridge. But we also discovered lots of tiny potted plants. These puzzled us, especially since I'd left explicit care instructions for my numerous, mature plants, which were nowhere to be seen. My annoyance turned to amusement, though, when I learned that after all my plants had died, the tenants organized a party to which each guest was required to bring a replacement. Hence the assortment of small cacti, ferns, and other grocery store greenery. I appreciated the attempt at restitution and chalked it up to the cost of going away.

The Struggle of Re-entry

In many respects, the hassles and expense related to getting your home back in shape are small potatoes compared with the emotional upheaval of re-entry. While most returnees will expect to have cleaning and repairs to do, few are prepared for the full, frontal assault that awaits them.

The term *re-entry* originates with the space program. Think of a small space capsule zooming into earth's atmosphere, aglow in flames – not an easy arrival! Neither is coming home after six to twelve months away. As much as you'd like to settle in smoothly and happily, it likely will be a far bumpier ride.

During those initial days, you'll begin to unpack and reconnect with people. There will be the joy of reunions with friends and family, the surprise of seeing how children have grown, and the excitement of being back in familiar surroundings. But despite the barrage of hugs and greetings, if the sabbatical has been a good one, something will seem very wrong. Instead of unmitigated joy, there may be a deep longing, even grieving, for the life you've left behind. Weeks after returning from our year in Oxford, all I felt was an incredible ache. I realized I'd put down roots that were so deep, they hurt when they were yanked out.

Too much stuff – I was distracted, of course. There were lots of errands for food and school supplies, an overnight trip to visit grandma, welcome home dinners, and the inevitable house repairs to deal with. I was also inundated by boxes. Having lived with so few possessions for a year, I found it distressing to realize just how much stuff we owned. I could relate to author Lynda

Cronin's (2000) comments after she returned from travelling for nine months:

> We've been unpacking the boxes in the basement and moving things upstairs. Where did it all come from? It's overwhelming. I thought we had shed everything before we left. What did the dishes do? Multiply in our absence? The contrast between what we have been happily used to living with and what we own is shocking. I'm embarrassed and made uncomfortable by our accumulation of objects. (p. 287)

After talking with other sabbatical returnees, I've learned that this is a very common reaction. Unfortunately, these feelings don't tend to be a catalyst for de-cluttering, since there's so much else to do upon return. Continues Cronin, "Most of it will just have to stay in the basement. We'll move up what we need for now and deal with the rest later" (p. 287). If she's anything like me, though, *later* will never come.

For example, I had a year's worth of mail to face. We'd asked our tenants to do a rough sort: to forward important personal letters and bills, recycle junk mail, and pile everything else (magazines, newsletters, and non-urgent letters and packages) in a container in one of the bedrooms. It was this overflowing box that greeted me. Some things could obviously be dumped, but a lot of items I wanted or needed to examine more carefully. I'm ashamed to say that while I read a few things right away, most of the pile was still there years after we returned.

Sleepwalking through re-entry – This initial sorting, unpacking, and socializing took place in a jet-lagged fog. On the first morning we were home, all four of us met in the bathroom at 3:25 a.m. saying, "You can't sleep either?" While the rest of the family adjusted in less than a week, it was a full ten days before I enjoyed a decent night's sleep. Feeling spacey became normal for me, and probably contributed to my feelings of discontent.

Yet it was more than discontent; I simply was not happy to be home. In fact, I kept referring to Oxford as "home." I had a real problem responding to comments like, "I bet you're glad to be back." An honest, "Not really," wasn't what others wanted to hear. However, those who had themselves gone on sabbaticals asked, "How are you adjusting to being home? Are you settling in OK?" They seemed to understand that we'd left a chunk of ourselves in England. Frankly, talking with people who've had similar experiences is probably the most helpful thing you can do for yourself during those first weeks. Not only will they listen to your feelings, they often are genuinely interested in hearing about your travels and adventures. This makes them unique.

While in England I'd told friends that once we were home, most people would ask how our year was. I'd then give a twenty-five-word response, and it would never come up again. Our English friends were appalled, but that was exactly what happened. Our children's friends were even blunter. Joshua found that no one wanted to hear about his year away, they just commented on how much he'd grown. One boy told him, "You missed a lot of stuff, like there are new rules for playing Manhunt [a variation of tag] at recess." Our sons quickly learned not to say too much, but at least their friends knew they'd been gone. One child returning from a year in Sweden was asked by a classmate, "Oh, you were away?"

It is sometimes hard to cope with such disinterest, but I've learned to limit my gushing to those twenty-five words or less, accepting that most people really don't care to know any more. If encouraged, I'd throw out a fun anecdote or even show some small photo albums, but I saved my real sharing for fellow sabbatical veterans – and my mother. She was the *only* person who patiently looked at all 61 rolls of film!

THE POST-SABBATICAL BLUES

W hile jet lag and a lack of interest in your experiences may contribute to general feelings of malaise, they're not the real problem. After each sabbatical, particularly following our year in Oxford, a cloud of melancholy descended on me that didn't lift for months. Each day at home simply paled in comparison with my sabbatical life. Nothing was as exciting, novel, stimulating, intense or as interesting as our time away.

Feeling "homesick" – A friend correctly diagnosed my problem: "Don't forget the well-known medical condition of 'post-sabbatical blues.' It is worse, the better the sabbatical has been." While the rest of the family had only mild symptoms, I suffered from a full-blown case after Oxford. My lack of purpose didn't help matters. When I returned from previous sabbaticals, I'd either started a new job or had a two-year-old to care for. But after my enormously satisfying role as homeschooling mum, I felt bereft when my children returned to the regular school system. The boys slipped easily into their classes, my husband dove into a busy university term, and there I sat, feeling miserable. I missed our close-knit family life. I missed biking into Oxford to hear evensong in a medieval chapel. I missed going on hikes with good friends. I missed our exciting weekend adventures. I wanted to go "home."

At one point while reciting my litany of laments to another sabbatical veteran, I asked how she had coped. Elsie laughed and said I'd better not follow her example, since she was depressed for a whole year. To keep her memories alive, she decided to organize the family's sabbatical photos, but that only compounded the problem. Like me, she particularly missed her family time together. Without overflowing calendars and conflicting schedules, parents and children on sabbatical simply have more time together. Individuals feel less pushing and pulling from outside forces, and instead turn to each other for conversation and activities.

New and deep friendships are another of the great joys, and therefore sad losses, of sabbaticals. These close bonds are often formed because we're disconnected from our usual support systems and have the time to invest in getting to know each other. This is true for children, too. When I interviewed sabbatical kids, they repeatedly said that the hardest part about heading home was leaving special friends. Some even returned the following year for a visit.

Finally, there's the inescapable fact that a sabbatical is a hard act to follow. Re-entry expert Craig Storti (2001) expresses this beautifully:

> Perhaps you went to Venice or the Red Sea or Masai Mara game park for the weekend, whereas now the choice is the movies, miniature golf or your aunt's house. On vacation you may have skied in the Alps, climbed Kilimanjaro, or gone to Bali. Now your options are to visit your parents in Cincinnati or your sister in Knoxville. It's not that you don't like going to the movies or won't enjoy seeing your sister; it's just that your leisure-time choices seem mundane and circumscribed. Life isn't as exciting as it used to be. (p. 34)

Gaining perspective – Of course, if you're honest, you can also remind yourself of some things that you *don't* miss. Once home I could walk down the street or participate in a conversation without fear of making a cultural gaffe. I no longer had any problems with foreign languages or accents – I understood everybody! And on each sabbatical there are usually idiosyncrasies that drive you nuts. For my husband, it was the Australian grocery carts with four independently turning wheels. He detested these and kept threatening to retrofit them with fixed rear wheels, so they could actually be steered! As for me, I distinctly remember the delight of shopping at a North American stationery store and buying a greeting card without someone exclaiming over my accent, asking if I was a tourist or how I liked Australia. A transaction that had taken fifteen to twenty minutes while on sabbatical, could now be executed in under sixty seconds. Amazing!

The flip side is no longer feeling "special." There's almost a celebrity status to being an obvious foreigner in some places, and I confess to sometimes enjoying that. The downside is never being allowed to be "normal" or a "local" during the entire time you're living overseas. I'm struck that at home I interact with lots of individuals whose accents are not like mine, but I never assume they're visitors. Canada is so multicultural that, instead, I expect that the owner of the Scottish, Nigerian or Slovakian accent lives here. But that wasn't my experience abroad. I'll never forget one time in an Aussie department store when a young clerk handed me my purchase and said, "Enjoy your stay!" Tired of months of this, I took the bag, smiled, and said, "I'm not a tourist; I live here," and walked away.

Reverse culture shock – Interestingly, it was shopping at home that caused me problems. I was immobilized by the choices of grapefruit juice (fifteen different kinds!), and felt stupid asking what a stamp cost. The clerk's accent also sounded wrong. Moments like these made me feel like a visitor in my own country, and I realized I was experiencing reverse culture shock – a reaction of surprise, confusion, and disorientation upon returning home.

I also suffered from the Rip van Winkle effect. While we were overseas, buildings had gone up, stores had closed, and people had moved away or died. Our neighbors had even built a fence in our absence, and then put their house up for sale. Noises, too, surprised me. I'd forgotten how loudly cicadas sang, and hearing a cardinal for the first time in a year was a real treat. There were habits to overcome as well. I continuously went to the wrong side of the car to drive, and I instinctively biked English-style on the left. More dangerous, though, was looking the wrong way when crossing the street. Thankfully, I lived to tell about it.

TRANSITION MODE

Confused, nostalgic, and grieving for your sabbatical life – not a pretty picture. However, there *are* a few things that you can do to ease your transition. After the first round of welcomes, you'll likely be expected to step right back into your pre-sabbatical life. Extended family members will want you to immediately resume particular responsibilities, at least visiting as before. This will be especially true if the brunt of care for elderly parents was borne by your siblings. They're ready to pass the baton, even if you aren't ready to receive it. Former committees will also be anticipating your return with glee. From their perspective, you've been on a long holiday and now it's time to get back to work. In both cases, you should plead for a period of adjustment before jumping back in. "Later" or even "no" may need to become part of your vocabulary.

Time for a change? – While you were away, you may have assessed your previous involvements and decided that you no longer want to continue some of them. (This obviously works better with committees than families!) Perhaps there's even something else you'd like to explore, a new sport, hobby, language or job. Sabbaticals offer not only a breather from your daily routines, but an opportunity to reflect on what you value and what really makes your heart sing.

So if at all possible, take your time before diving into your previous activities and commitments. Postpone decisions until you begin to adjust and feel normal again, which may take a few months. Don't feel pushed to unpack the house immediately either. One couple was home for six weeks before starting on their boxes, choosing an unstressed, "so what?" approach to settling in. There were simply more important things to do first, like visiting new grandchildren and buying a car. The garden will also keep, unless you find weeding therapeutic.

In other words, be kind to yourself and keep your expectations low. If you're feeling overwhelmed, easily distracted, and prone to frittering hours and days, know that you're in good company. Just remember, time is on your side.

Settled at Last

Eventually, you'll start to really enjoy aspects of being home. My husband re-connected via local corn-on-the-cob, and each weekday I looked forward to listening to a favorite radio program I'd missed while away. I began admitting that it *was* good to be back in our house, especially after I finally excavated most of the rooms. Broken appliances were repaired and our calendar started to fill up. Life was beginning to return to normal, although a friend reminded me that "normal" is just a setting on the dryer.

Keeping the sabbatical flame burning – I may have settled in, but I wasn't ready to let go of our sabbatical life. After each time away, I've consciously tried to incorporate some of our experiences. Following our year in England, I instituted afternoon tea when the boys came home from school, a tradition they really enjoyed. I started riding my bike more, after a year of using one constantly in Oxford. Due to all that biking overseas, I'd shifted to using a backpack instead of a purse, a habit I've continued. (I do break down and carry a handbag for weddings and funerals, though.) We bought a front-loading washing machine after having one in Oxford, convinced of its washing superiority and water conservation. I also got so used to the glorious smell of air-dried sheets in Switzerland (where we didn't have a dryer), that I've hung out laundry ever since.

I had also become quite enamored with thrift shops while in England, so I sought them out at home. In fact, I joined our university's International Student Orientation Team to share my knowledge of where to buy things cheaply with new students. And while we had always enjoyed getting to know visitors from around the world, we now make a point of extending dinner invitations to international students, especially at Thanksgiving and

Christmas. We know firsthand how nice it is to be invited into someone's home and to learn more about local culture and traditions.

There are other ways to keep the sabbatical alive. Some people continue language lessons after returning home. Others subscribe to foreign newspapers or magazines. One family even changed the way they celebrated Christmas after spending their sabbatical in Stockholm more than twenty-five years ago. Each December Shirley and Jay Thomson drive three hours round-trip to a Swedish Christmas Fair to buy authentic candles and assorted delicacies, including special smoked herring that they enjoy on Christmas Eve. While they still serve a regular Christmas Day meal, they added this celebration on the 24th because that's how it's done in Scandinavia. Ever since their sabbatical, their tree has had traditional Swedish decorations of straw and wood, with white electric lights (they drew the line at candles on branches). As well, special Swedish Advent candles grace their mantel, another tradition they brought from Stockholm.

Impact on children – Our boys very naturally integrated their overseas experiences into their school assignments. In second grade Joshua chose to do a project on the crimson rosella, one of Australia's colorful birds. He included a photograph of some eating out of his hand, and showed off his rosella puppet on the day of his report. Having witnessed culinary historians prepare a Tudor feast in the kitchens of Henry VIII's Hampton Court Palace, our oldest son gave a presentation on Tudor cooking in History. He even decided to use Tudor recipes to fulfill a cooking requirement for a junior high Family Studies class. Once home, the Rempel children drew upon their sabbatical experiences Down Under for their poetry assignments, as well as using Australian themes in their art projects and even French speeches. Another family's sabbatical in France had such a profound effect on one daughter that she decided to major in French in university. She later returned to that country to study and live. Not surprisingly, author Kenneth Zahorski (1994) believes, "A good sabbatical, like a good book, has the power to change one's life" (p. 115). So never underestimate the impact of a sabbatical on your children – or yourself!

If you want to preserve the enjoyable aspects of your sabbatical, consider these additional suggestions:

- **Stay in touch with friends** – If, like us, your address book grows after each sabbatical, help keep your memories alive by maintaining those relationships. Besides sending letters and email, every so often surprise overseas friends with a phone call.
- **Enjoy your photos** – One family made their favorite shots into a screensaver. They remembered their wonderful adventure each time they sat down at the computer. Lower-tech photo albums and scrapbooks also have their place. In addition, consider enlarging your pictures. I took a marvelous shot of our two boys wearing black berets on a cobblestone street in Paris. It is my quintessential sabbatical photo, so I had it blown-up and mounted, and it hangs in our dining room as a continual reminder of our year away.

- **Reminisce with your family** – Photos are great catalysts for "I remember" moments. Enjoy retelling anecdotes and traveller's tales. (Heaven knows no one else wants to hear them!) But seriously, you've built a treasure-trove of memories – savor them.
- **Continue the family adventures** – While you won't be able to keep up the weekly excursions you enjoyed on sabbatical, perhaps one outing a month might be possible. I confess that after every sabbatical I start out with great intentions, and then real life elbows in. How I miss those Sunday afternoon hikes, the trips to museums, and "Expotitions" à la Pooh. So do as I say, not as I do, and recapture some of the delight of your sabbatical by wrestling a spot in your calendar and going away with your family for a day.

A final thought – One sabbatical veteran said that sabbaticals aren't better or worse than normal life, just different. I disagree; I definitely think they are better. Sabbaticals are regular life lifted beyond the routine, where relationships and priorities can be seen more clearly, and where spending extensive, enjoyable time together is as easy as breathing. Just as concentrated orange juice is stronger than regular juice, for me, sabbaticals are concentrated life. No wonder I miss them and can't wait for our next opportunity to live overseas. After all, the best antidote for the post-sabbatical blues is planning the next one!

REFERENCES

Cronin, L. (2000). *Midlife runaway: A grown up's guide to taking a year off*. Toronto: Macmillan Canada.

Foreign Affairs and International Trade Canada, *Sample Consent Letter*. Retrieved May 1, 2008, from http://www.voyage.gc.ca/main/before/consent_letter-en.asp

Huss, E. C. (2002). *Love that lasts: Personal stories of lasting marriage*. Kitchener, ON: Pandora Press.

Kohls, L. R. (2001). *Survival kit for overseas living: For Americans planning to live and work abroad* (4th ed.). Yarmouth, ME: Intercultural Press.

Lanigan, C. (2002). *Travel with children* (4th ed.). Footscray, Australia: Lonely Planet.

Lansky, V. (2004). *Trouble-free travel with children: Over 700 helpful hints for parents on the go* (3rd ed.). Minnetonka, MN: Book Peddlers.

Messner, N. S. (1991). *Your key to vacation apartments in London*. Bedford, MA: Mills and Sanderson.

Morrison, Alison. Sensational Sabbatical Suggestions: Sabbatical Travel Tips for Planning Temporary Employment Away from Home. Retrieved Feb. 4, 2004, from http://omni.cc.purdue.edu/~alltson/sabbl.htm

Pascoe, R. (1998a). *Culture shock! A parent's guide*. Singapore: Times Editions.

Pascoe, R. (1998b). *Culture shock! A wife's guide*. Portland: Graphic Arts Center.

Portnoy, S., & Portnoy, J. (1995). *How to take great trips with your kids* (rev. ed.). Boston: Harvard Press.

Rabe, M. (1997). *Culture shock! Living and working abroad*. Portland: Graphic Arts Center.

Storti, C. (2001). *The art of coming home* (rev. ed.). Yarmouth, ME: Intercultural Press.

Zahorski, K. J. (1994). *The sabbatical mentor: A practical guide to successful sabbaticals*. Bolton, MA: Anker Publishing.

Appendix A
Table of Contents for

The Tenants' Guide:
The Source of All Knowledge
for 123 Any Street

(A template to be adapted by sabbatical families
to reflect the requirements of their homes)

By John and Jane Homeowner

Note: The *Tenants' Guide* is a reference for those who will be living in the family's home while they are away on sabbatical, and includes instructions regarding house care, mail, utilities, etc. The full template is available at

www.newforums.com/sabbaticals101.

APPENDIX B
RESOURCES AND RECOMMENDED READING – AN ANNOTATED BIBLIOGRAPHY

Axtell, R. E. (Ed.). (1993). *Do's and taboos around the world* (3rd ed.). New York: Wiley. Tips on appropriate body language, greetings, gift giving, attire, and more for most countries of the world. Geared toward business travellers, but still helpful and interesting.

Graf, D. (2000). *Point it: Picture dictionary travellers' language kit* (7th ed.). Munich: Graf Editions. An answer to the prayers of the linguistically-challenged! Simply point to the color photos of food, accommodation options, toilets, etc., for instant communication around the world.

Guterson, D. (1992). *Family matters: Why homeschooling makes sense.* New York: Harcourt Brace Jovanovich. A beautifully written, inspiring place to start for anyone considering do-it-yourself education while on sabbatical, by homeschooling dad and author of *Snow Falling on Cedars*.

Harriman, C. W. (2007). *Take your kids to Europe: How to travel safely (and sanely) in Europe with your children* (8th ed.). Guilford, CT: Globe Pequot Press. Detailed and entertaining advice on planning, executing, and enjoying an extended family trip to Europe, including *The Totally Biased Guide to What to See and Do* in over a dozen countries.

Hess, M. B., & Linderman, P. (2007). *The expert expat: Your guide to successful relocation abroad* (rev. ed.). Yarmouth, ME: Nicholas Brealey/Intercultural Press. A thorough guide to overseas moves, especially for long-term placements with sponsoring organizations (military, Foreign Service, etc.).

Lanigan, C. (2002). *Travel with children* (4th ed.). Footscray, Australia: Lonely Planet. Honest, amusing anecdotes (e.g., *Nappies on the Silk Road* and *Pregnant Backpacking*) interspersed with practical information on the availability of disposable diapers, things to do in each country listed, and suggestions for enriching the experience. A treat to read.

Lansky, V. (2004). *Trouble-free travel with children: Over 700 helpful hints for parents on the go* (3rd ed.). Minnetonka, MN: Book Peddlers. Humorous, extremely helpful, and without doubt the best book on the subject.

Newman, E. (2000). *Going abroad: The bathroom survival guide* (2nd ed.). St. Paul, MN: Marlor Press. More than you'll ever want to know about the toilets of the world and how to use them, from squat versions to futuristic kiosks on European streets. Fun and helpful.

Pascoe, R. (2000). *Homeward bound: A spouse's guide to repatriation.* North Vancouver: Expatriate Press. A thorough and chatty discussion of the under-appreciated struggle of returning home, including such concerns as the re-entering, job-hunting spouse. Directed to those who've spent years abroad, often in developing countries, but offers useful insights.

Pascoe, R. (2002). *Culture shock! A wife's guide* (expanded ed.). Portland: Graphic Arts Center. Originally titled *A Broad Abroad*, the book is touted as "a self-help emotional guidebook for the travelling wife," especially those on extended diplomatic or business postings. Enjoyable and practical.

Pascoe, R. (2006). *Raising global nomads: Parenting abroad in an on-demand world.* North Vancouver: Expatriate Press. Seasoned advice from the "Expat Expert" about the joys and challenges of raising children overseas. Also covers pregnancy and childbirth abroad, and the unique world of Third Culture Kids.

Piet-Pelon, N. J., & Hornby, B. (1992). *Women's guide to overseas living* (2nd ed.). Yarmouth, ME: Intercultural Press. Particularly good for those heading to developing countries for multi-year placements. Extensive sections on helping children adjust and advice for women seeking employment.

Portnoy, S., & Portnoy, J. (1995). *How to take great trips with your kids* (rev. ed.). Boston: Harvard Press. Helpful tips on planning, packing, and getting to one's destination. Includes chapters on child development and travel at different ages, plus an impressive collection of more than fifty games that can be played en route to keep boredom at bay.

Rabe, M. (1997). *Culture shock! Living and working abroad.* Portland: Graphic Arts Center. Solid advice, especially for those planning long-term assignments in developing countries. Includes suggestions on evaluating Third World housing, domestic help, hygiene, plus an overview of common tropical diseases, drugs, terrorism, and even preparations for evacuation. On a lighter note, *A Note to Your Dog – To Go or Not To Go*, is actually addressed to man's best friend.

Simony, M. (Ed.). (1993). *The traveler's reading guide: Ready-made reading lists for the armchair traveler* (rev. ed.). New York: Facts On File. What a find! Pithy, thumbnail sketches of background reading, history, and especially novels grouped by country and continent. A marvelous resource for the literate traveller.

Storti, C. (2001). *The art of coming home* (rev. ed.). Yarmouth, ME: Intercultural Press. An enjoyable examination of re-entry, primarily after prolonged, overseas experiences by business people, exchange students, Peace Corps volunteers, military personnel, missionaries, and their families. Excellent general suggestions and anecdotes, though, plus a look at the special problems of returning teens.

Williamson, D. T. (2004). *2005 Tax and financial guide for college teachers and other college personnel.* College Park, MD: Academic Information Service. Includes American tax advice regarding sabbaticals, and seems to be updated only when there are major changes in the tax law.

Zahorski, K. J. (1994). *The sabbatical mentor: A practical guide to successful sabbaticals.* Bolton, MA: Anker Publishing. The perfect companion to my book, offering guidance on the professional hoops academics must jump through in order to plan, apply for, and pursue a sabbatical. Provides persuasive arguments for these periods of professional renewal, rejuvenation, and research, as well as helpful samples of sabbatical applications and reports.

WEB-BASED RESOURCES

Canadian Association of University Teachers (www.caut.ca) – produces an annual CAUT Income Tax Guide for Canadian academics. Available in pdf format, one section deals specifically with sabbatical leaves.

Canadian Consular Affairs (www.voyage.gc.ca) – country-by-country visa requirements, consular information, travel warnings, advice on travelling with children, and reports on conditions in 223 countries.

Canadian Passport Office (www.ppt.gc.ca) – easy-to-navigate information on fees, forms, renewal, travel tips, and useful links.

CARES (www.kidsflysafe.com) – avoid hauling a car seat on board airplanes by using CARES (Child Aviation Restraint System), the alternative, belt-and-buckle child restraint. It's for use only on aircraft (NOT in cars), for children one and older, weighing 22 to 44 lbs (10-20 kg). I've not tried this device personally (since it was invented long after my sons needed car seats), but it's been approved by the FAA and Transport Canada, and has won many parent and product awards.

Centers for Disease Control and Prevention (www.cdc.gov/travel/) – this well-respected, Atlanta-based institution lists recommended immunization and health concerns by country. Includes a section on travel with children, as well as helpful advice like "Boil it, cook it, peel it or forget it!" (404) 332-4559.

Culture Shock! series (www.gacpc.com) – includes enlightening, country-specific guides to culture and customs, published by the Graphic Arts Center. Order online or request a catalogue, (800) 452-3032.

Expat Expert (www.expatexpert.com) – an impressive website by author Robin Pascoe. Includes articles about expatriate life (going abroad, living abroad, and coming home), excerpts from her books, and extensive links to expat groups, useful books, and sites on international medical, career, and parenting issues.

Insure My Trip (www.insuremytrip.com) – online insurance broker that offers policy comparisons of international, expatriate health insurance.

International Youth Hostel Federation (www.hihostels.com) – also known as Hostelling International (HI), provides a worldwide directory and almost anything else you'd like to know about hostelling.

Kodak (www.kodak.com) – search for "airport security x-rays" for recommendations on film and flying.

Lonely Planet (www.lonelyplanet.com) – super travel information site includes an online shop for LP's incomparable guidebooks, as well as updates, interviews, and photos. Check out the Thorn Tree travellers' forum, a lively, informative (and addictive) bulletin board that is subdivided by destination.

Magellan's (www.magellans.com) – a wide selection of traveller's supplies, including wonderful money belts, electrical adapters, and international surge protection products for your computer. Order via the website or their excellent catalogue, (800) 962-4943.

Sabbatical Homes (www.sabbaticalhomes.com) – international matchmaking for sabbatical housing, begun in 2000 by an academic spouse. No fee to place a home-wanted ad, only a very reasonable charge to post your property. I have no experience with this California-based company, but was impressed by the numerous and effusive testimonials listed, especially from repeat customers.

Skype (www.skype.com) – skip phone bills and use this Internet telephony software to contact friends and relatives. Besides a free Skype account, you'll need broadband, plus a microphone and speakers, or better yet, a headset. There are other VoIP (Voice over Internet Protocol) programs, such as Google Talk, MSN, and Jabber, but Skype is probably the best known.

STA (www.statravel.com) – a worldwide travel agency with a major American focus, specializing in student travel. STA sells regular and long-stay tickets, accommodations, and discount student and teacher ID cards (ISIC and ITIC). Locate the office nearest you, (800) 777-0112.

Tales From a Small Planet (www.talesmag.com) – an online, expat magazine with lots of travellers' tales and advice, as well as links to resources. The list of international educational options, under "schools," is particularly good.

Travel Cuts (www.travelcuts.com) – Canada's national student travel agency, also useful for budget travellers. Offers particularly good deals on year-long flights and sells discount ID cards (ISIC and ITIC). Locate the office nearest you, (800) 954-2666.

Travel With Your Kids (www.travelwithyourkids.com) – a fantastic site by a couple who've lived around the world with their children. Topics include planning, flying, jet lag, hotel safety, toilets, moving abroad, recommended books, and an incredible array of useful links.

U.S. State Department (www.state.gov/travel) – a great, all-purpose stop for Americans travelling and living abroad. Sections include passports, visas, country background notes, travel warnings, and helpful links, plus information on American and international schools through the Office of Overseas Schools.

ABOUT THE AUTHOR

Nancy Matthews is a freelance travel writer and the mother of two sons. Born and raised on the U.S. west coast, she married a Canadian statistics professor and has lived in the Great White North ever since. Thanks to her husband's sabbaticals, she has had the opportunity to experience life in various corners of the world. Their first sabbatical was in London and Berne, Switzerland, followed by an exchange in Newcastle, NSW, Australia. They loved life Down Under so much, they returned for two more sabbaticals in the same location. Another special highlight was a year spent in Oxford, England, where they homeschooled their boys. She and her family call Kitchener, Ontario, home when they're not exploring the world.

The author and family at Sovereign Hill, Victoria, Australia.
[Photo credit: Red Hill Photographic Rooms]

INDEX

W

websites
    make your own 96
    web-based resources 145-147
    website for the *Tenants' Guide*
    template 11, 141

wills 55-56
working, *see* employment

Z

Zahorski, Kenneth 135, 145